Heal My Broken Heart

An LDS Guide to Dealing With Those Bound by the Deadly Sin of Pornography

Ruth Davidson
Tamara Davies

Gatehouse
MEDIA

Gatehouse Media
367 W. 1450 N.
American Fork, Utah 84003

Heal My Broken Heart

ISBN: 0-9743621-0-7

HISTORY
2nd Edition: Summer 2004

PRINTED IN THE UNITED STATES OF AMERICA.
10 9 8 7 6 5 4 3 2 1

Cover Design by
Jon Madsen
2812 N 600 E
Lehi, UT 84043
jmadsen@hotmail.com

I am me.
I belong to no one but God.
He has given me life,
strength and peace of mind.
With His help I can do all that I need to do
to live this life in beauty,
dignity,
and service to Him.
With His help—and His alone—
I will become what I was born to be:
a daughter of God,
a blessing to my family,
my friends and mankind.
The power is within me—
A gift from God,
a precious gift.
I will not leave Him.
I will follow His lead.
His strength is mine.
Forever. . .

—a "Psalm" given from Heaven
to a woman in one of her darkest
hours

Contents

NOTE

Names carrying an asterisk (*) are not real and are intended to maintain the anonymity of the person(s) involved in the examples and stories herein.

Heal My Broken Heart

An LDS Guide to Dealing With Those Bound by the Deadly Sin of Pornography

Ruth Davidson
Tamara Davies

1

Pornography: A Deadly Sin

A pernicious, venomous plague is sweeping over the earth in ever-increasing intensity, infecting the inhabitants with its deadly poison. It is leaving behind countless victims and untold destruction, devastating individuals and families caught in its terrible wake. Many are suffering greatly because of it. This noxious plague is pornography in all of its lethal, toxic forms.

Members of the Church of Jesus Christ of Latter-day Saints are not immune to this widespread epidemic. Growing numbers of Church members have become caught in the flood of filth and are now grappling with the devastation and heartache brought on by participation in this great sin.

As Elder Richard G. Scott has stated, "One of the most damning influences on earth, one that has caused uncountable grief, suffering, heartache, and destroyed marriages is the onslaught of pornography in all of its vicious, corroding, destructive forms. Whether it be through the printed page, movies, television, obscene lyrics, the telephone, or on a flickering personal computer screen, pornography is overpoweringly addictive and severely damaging. This potent tool of Lucifer degrades the mind, heart, and soul of any who use it. All who are caught in its seductive, tantalizing web and remain so, will become addicted to its immoral, destructive influence." (*Ensign*, May 2000, p. 36) The tool of pornography is truly one of Satan's "cunning plans which he hath devised to ensnare the hearts of men." (Alma 28:13)

We boldly affirm that pornography has become one of the most common precursors to all sexual sins, sins which include masturbation, fornication, adultery, child abuse, participation in prostitution, homosexuality, sexually deviant behaviors, crimes or any other sexual perversions. All these iniquities, in any form, create deep, searing wounds for not only transgressors but those closely associated with them. Pornography can truly be considered the gate which, once opened, "blindeth the eyes, and hardeneth the hearts of the children of men, and leadeth them away into broad roads, that they perish and are lost." (1 Nephi 12:17)

This book is meant to be a guide to help bring needed healing and strength to friends and families of those transgressors who have allowed pornography to permeate their lives and homes. The trials that have come into their lives because of the consequences of those making these grave eternal choices will be some of the deepest and severe they will have to pass through. The intense betrayal and devastating emotions they will experience are real and agonizing. There will be deep wounds inflicted on their souls, injuries that can only be overcome through the sustaining power and strength of the healer of all wounds, our Lord and Savior, Jesus Christ. He has suffered untold agony so that He might know "the weakness of man and how to succor them who are tempted." (D&C 62: 1) Only He can impart the "word which healeth the wounded soul" (Jacob 2:8) to those who bear the unjust burdens of one who has become enslaved to the terrible addiction of pornography.

2

A Powerful Addiction

The Parable of the Yard Fire

There was a man who, after a late spring storm, decided it was time to burn the cluttered branches and excess wood in his yard. He gathered his son and three other young men to help him with this task. Because the wood and branches had been soaked from the storm, he knew he needed help to get the fire going. He went into the garage and got what he thought would be similar to lighter fluid—a can of camping fuel, and then poured it abundantly over the mass of branches. Little did he know that this camping fuel (what some people term "white gas" because of its evaporative nature) was highly flammable and extremely dangerous. Without reading the instructions on the can, he bent over the fire and attempted to start it with a lighter. After three clicks of the lighter, only a small, scarcely noticeable spark was produced.

In an instant, that spark created a flame that literally exploded upward, engulfing the man's head and upper torso. The skin on his face and head were burned; his hair and brows were singed; even his ears became blistered and red. The boys were close by the fire and barely missed the effects of this combustible flame.

Reeling in pain, the man left the fire and went inside to get his wife to check the extent of damage done to him. As they were speaking and wondering what to do with his injuries, his wife suddenly asked what had happened to the fire. Had he put it out? When they realized he had not, his wife quickly went outside only to find the boys playing with and feeding the fire. After a sharp demand to stop what they were doing, she went back in to check on her husband.

As his pain deepened and continued, they decided they needed to seek medical help in overcoming his injuries. They called the doctor and made an appointment. A short time later, the man had in hand a powerfully addictive medication to help him overcome the pain of his burn. He had also been given a severe warning by the doctor: Anyone who had suffered a burn such as he needed to be extremely careful about any exposure to the sun, especially during the year following his injury. He needed to be vigilant in guarding his skin from the sun's dangerous rays. He also received the forewarning that because of what had happened, he would be vulnerable to skin cancer for the rest of his life.

Another interesting occurrence happened during the weeks following his exposure to the fire. At first, the extent of his injuries had not been fully apparent. However, after one week his head and face became a deep, dark red; there were even white shadows around his eyes where he had closed them. This skin soon peeled off. As he neared the second week, even the skin that had not been burned as severely began peeling off. These were injuries he had not known he had sustained.

This man's son came in some time later with the can of camping fuel and read the "Warning" to him. It said, "DANGER: Extremely flammable. Harmful or fatal if swallowed. If not used properly, this fuel can cause flash fires and serious burn injuries. Fuel vapors are explosive, invisible and can be ignited by sparks, flames or other ignition sources many feet away."

And finally, "Keep out of reach of children."

How like pornography this parable of the fire is. One exposure—*one*—can bring lasting injury to the soul of the man who participates in it. The ensuing damage, especially if an addiction follows, can be deep, extensive, and take much time and extreme effort to overcome. Furthermore, there can be a vulnerability to pornography that lasts throughout a lifetime, even when the superficial healing of the wound is over and done.

Pornography also, as the parable illustrates, can be a danger to the innocent people who are around it—whether or not they participate in pornography themselves or are the victims of those who engage in it. Like the victims of second-hand cigarette smoke, these innocent people are literally subjected to the evils and darkness brought in around them and breathe polluted spiritual air.

Truly, the warning regarding pornography should read: "DANGER: Extremely flammable. Spiritually harmful or fatal if swallowed. This fuel can cause flash fires and serious burn injuries to the soul. Fuel vapors are explosive, invisible and can be ignited by sparks, flames or other ignition sources many feet away." And finally, "Keep out of reach of children."

"Eyes Full of Adultery. . .That Cannot Cease From Sin" (2nd Peter 2:14)

Many powerful forces are at work in the enslaving addiction of pornography.

• Chemicals Within our Bodies

Mark Chamberlain in his book *Wanting More: The Challenge of Enjoyment in the Age of Addiction* speaks about the chemicals in our bodies that are released in response to our various experiences in life. Even in infancy, "certain forms of stimulation have been shown to release endorphins and increase the activity of the pleasure chemical dopamine," he claims. (p. 47)

Studies have shown that there are indeed narcotic-type receptors in the human brain. The brain has its own "opium-like messengers" that "abound where sensory input is processed"—in our senses of sight, hearing, taste, smell and touch. (p. 48)

Chamberlain states:

> Substances and behaviors become addictive precisely to the extent that they trigger or mimic the body's own chemicals and activate our natural reward system. It is an emotional jolt, and can be a "thrill," to take our bodies. . .and subject them to stimulation that overwhelms. . . .The same sexual responsiveness sensitive enough that we can appreciate a soft touch or the mere sight of our spouse can also be overloaded by the sight of sculpted bodies in provocative poses.
>
> . . .After we subject ourselves to an artificially intense degree of stimulation, we become increasingly insensitive to such stimulation, and the intensity must be increased even more to have the same effect. . . .This is the paradoxical nature of the cycle of addiction: We add more and more stimulation only to find that it does less and less for us. (pp. 23-25)

Pornography is powerfully addictive solely due to these chemical reactions in the body. It is no wonder that one man claimed, as he was attempting to go through a repentance process, that he "would sweat bullets" whenever he passed a place where he had received previous pornographic stimulation.

Steven A. Cramer, in *The Worth of a Soul*, describes the powerful addiction to pornography this way:

> The grip of this awful desire was so great that when I passed an adult magazine stand, or saw

someone reading such magazines, I would break into
a cold sweat. My body would tremble, and my face
would turn white. My heart would pound madly,
and I would be totally consumed with desire. The
only way to survive the onslaught of such attacks
was to turn and literally run from the area. But even
if I was successful in my escape, I would be haunted
for days, wondering what I had missed. (p. 9)

Truly, as our church leaders claim, pornography is as
addictive as drugs or alcohol. Even one exposure to this deadly
sin can lead one to a broken life fraught with pain, heartache
and despair.

• **Intergenerational Tendencies**
We are all aware of the fact that many traits are
passed down from generation to generation—from mental or
emotional illnesses to predispositions toward alcoholism or
other addictions. Physical, emotional and sexual abuse can also
be traced intergenerationally. It is not hard to infer from this
that a tendency or predisposition toward sexual sin, such as
participation in pornography or other sexual sins, can also be
passed from one generation to the next.

Intergenerational sins were described by the Lord in the
Pearl of Great Price. "For these many generations. . .have they gone
astray," He tells us, "and have denied me, and have sought their
own counsels in the dark; and in their own abominations. . .have
not kept the commandments." (Moses 6:28)

To take the intergenerational test, look at the lives of
immediate and extended family members—fathers, mothers,
brothers, sisters, grandparents, their parents, aunts, uncles,
cousins, etc. Is there a tendency toward sexual problems
throughout the family? One woman, who discovered her
husband had been extensively involved in pornography since his
early teenage years, realized in shocked amazement that sexual
problems had been prevalent throughout his family: sexual

sins before missions and marriages, affairs during marriages, addictions to pornography, inappropriate relationships with others while married, etc. Only when she saw the pervasiveness of these sexual sins did she realize how these problems had been spread intergenerationally throughout the family line.

The reason for these intergenerational traits is twofold. First of all, genetic tendencies—those traits and behaviors which we are subject to because of our physiological makeup—play a powerful role in our lives and strongly contribute to our behavior and characteristics. Secondly, and probably more importantly, our natures and spirits are subject to the environment in which they are brought up—not solely to the physical but the spiritual environment, as well.

This "spiritual environment" is as real—and probably more powerfully damaging—than the physical environment to which someone is subject. The reason damage can occur from a spiritually polluted background has a specific basis. Just as the Lord has certain emissaries for righteousness, so, too, do Satan and his forces have specific emissaries for evil and darkness. In other words, certain evil spirits accompany certain sins. This would explain consistent patterns of thought—patterns of excuses and deceit, patterns of lies or behavior, patterns of anger and rage against righteousness, etc.—that accompany sin.

When there is wickedness brought into a home—or prevailing wickedness that has been passed down intergenerationally, the transgressor and the innocent parties in that home are literally "surrounded by demons, yea, . . .are encircled about by the angels of him who hath sought to destroy. . .souls." (Helaman 13:37) When these spirits are allowed in because of the misuse of agency, these spirits can and will cause extensive damage to whomever they come in contact with, intruding on the agency of the innocent parties in the home.

As President Ezra Taft Benson has stated, "Children are born innocent, not evil. They are not sent to earth, however, to neutral environments. They are sent to homes that, for good or evil, influence their ideas, emotions, thoughts, and standards, by which future choices will be made." (*Ensign*, May 1981, p. 34)

It is no wonder that in places where there have been sexual or other transgressions, many severe problems for other family members exist within the same home. Issues such as depression, intense or hidden aggression, emotional problems, inappropriate behavioral problems, social maladjustment, exacerbated learning difficulties, feelings of insecurity or inadequacy, intense preoccupation with superficial things—such as beauty, weight or wealth—to create feelings of worth, and even the tendency toward the same sins or transgressions often abound. The evil spirits they have been exposed to are powerfully destructive and, when left unchecked within a home or family, cause extensive damage that can be both devastating and debilitating to those innocent parties.

These evil spirits have an even more powerful grip if the innocent parties in the home are physically or sexually abused by transgressors. The damage done by these abuses is sometimes so powerful that this evil continues to perpetuate itself for generations. No wonder victims of these terrible assaults often suffer irreparable damage. When there is a healing, it is only through the Savior's atonement and it often takes years of heartache and suffering to complete.

• Our Carnal Natures

The desires of our carnal natures is another reason pornography can become highly addictive. As the scriptures state, "All men that are in a state of nature, or I would say, in a carnal state, are in the gall of bitterness and in the bonds of iniquity; they are without God in the world, and they have gone contrary to the nature of God; therefore, they are in a state contrary to the nature of happiness." (Alma 41:11) Many of us are battling our fallen natures in trying to overcome pornography and lust for the things of this world.

This lesson was brought home to one woman, who in her life struggled with feelings of inadequacy and a lack of self-esteem. She noted a time in her scripture reading when she had a difficult time with King Benjamin's final sermon to his people. It sometimes seemed abrasive and harsh to her vulnerable feelings, especially when he said such things as, "Can ye say aught of yourselves? . . .Nay. Ye cannot say that ye are even as much as the dust of the earth." (Mosiah 2:25) He also spoke of peoples' "nothingness, and [their] worthless and fallen state" (Mosiah 4:5) and called them "unworthy creatures." (Mosiah 4:11) These seemed to add to her feelings of inferiority and dejection.

Only when she tied these expressions into what King Benjamin truly meant—that he was speaking about the "carnal state" of man (Mosiah 4:2) and not the eternal part of our beings—did she begin to see King Benjamin's words in the right perspective. For "the natural man is an enemy to God, and has been from the fall of Adam, and will be, forever and ever, unless he yields to the enticings of the Holy Spirit, and putteth off the natural man." (Mosiah 3:19) ❧

Steven R. Cramer in his book, *Putting on the Armor of God,* described it this way: "The fact that evil sometimes appeals to us does not prove that we are unworthy. It is just a normal part of mortality. We all recognize the truth of President Kimball's words: 'Because men and women are human and normally carnally minded. . .to do evil is usually easier than to do right.' If we would win our battles with temptation we must recognize that the Lord does not reject people because of their fallen nature, but invites them to come to him for a new heart." (p. 88)

Paul in the *New Testament* says it like this:

> For we know that the law is spiritual: but I am carnal, sold under sin.
> For that which I do I allow not: for what I would, that do I not; but what I hate, that do I.

> . . .For I know that in me (that is, in my
> flesh,) dwelleth no good thing; for to will is present
> with me; but how to perform that which is good I
> find not.
>> . . .I delight in the law of God after the
> inward man:
>> But I see another law in my members,
> warring against the law of my mind, and bringing
> me into captivity to the law of sin which is in my
> members.
>> O wretched man that I am! (Romans 7:15-24)

Truly, our carnal natures are a powerful force in the struggle against pornography and can only be overcome when hearts and minds become open to the redeeming power of our Lord and Savior, Jesus Christ.

• Personal Weaknesses and Vulnerabilities

Oftentimes personal weaknesses and vulnerabilities can contribute to a person's tendency toward an addiction to pornography. Sometimes these weaknesses come from a transgressor's background or deficiencies from the past, even when sexual sin is not necessarily present in the home. For instance, in many cases when transgressors have not received unconditional (gratifying) love as a child, they often seek for that gratification elsewhere. A childhood filled with this lack of love, with manipulation or control, with deceit or intolerance, with impatience, abuse or neglect often breeds the kind of aching emptiness that makes one look outward to other sources for fulfillment. One man, in trying to understand some of the factors that might have contributed to his addiction to pornography, could see plainly that he was not loved unconditionally in his past. Like many others, he tried to mask his intense need for love and acceptance through his addiction.

Other times weaknesses and vulnerabilities become apparent when we have not been given the right tools to deal with negative emotions such as anger, frustration, depression, lack of self-esteem, lack of self-confidence, worry, sorrow, discouragement, fear, etc. This can also contribute to a tendency to look to pornography for escape or temporary fulfillment.

The Lord often gives us weaknesses, as well, and He many times places us in families or circumstances that will give rise to these weaknesses. He says this: "If men come unto me I will show unto them their weakness. *I give unto men weakness that they may be humble*; and my grace is sufficient for all men that humble themselves before me; for if they humble themselves before me, and have faith in me, then will I make weak things become strong unto them." (Ether 12:27, italics added) Weaknesses and vulnerabilities are often a gift from the Lord, then, that we might come to know Him and taste of His redeeming grace and power by overcoming those weaknesses through His mercy.

Paul talked about his weaknesses this way:

> And lest I should be exalted above measure through the abundance of the revelations, there was given to me a thorn in the flesh, the messenger Satan to buffet me, lest I should be exalted above measure.
>
> For this thing I besought the Lord thrice, that it might depart from me.
>
> And he said unto me, My grace is sufficient for thee: for my strength is made perfect in weakness. Most gladly therefore will I rather glory in my infirmities, that the power of Christ may rest upon me. (2nd Corinthians 12:7-9)

• Masturbation

Masturbation is a powerful addiction in and of itself and is often a precursor to or follows pornography addictions, contributing to pornography's overpowering influence. Though masturbation is many times a manifestation of sexual problems, it is also a manifestation of non-sexual problems.

Steven A. Cramer has made this statement about masturbation:

> Many are held captive in this addiction because it has become a . . .method of coping with *non-sexual* problems covering a wide spectrum of social inadequacies. . . .For example, masturbation is often used as an attempt to escape from the stresses of academic, employment, marital or family problems, feelings of loneliness, discouragement and depression. For some it provides a quick sedative for sleep. Subconsciously it is used by many in an attempt to compensate for the feelings of inadequacy, lack of self-worth and even as a form of self-punishment for feelings of unworthiness. (*Putting on the Armor of God*, p. 135)

It is critical to note that though masturbation is not always accompanied by the viewing of pornography, the viewing of pornography is almost inevitably accompanied by masturbation. It becomes not a matter of "if" but "when." Masturbation is most often the means of release for those exposed to Satan's cunning entrapments.

Pornography—A "Secret Abomination" (Alma 37:27)

As shown from the above examples, pornography, a "secret abomination," can become a powerful addiction based on many different physical, emotional, mental, social and spiritual factors. The combination of the enticements of evil spirits, the artificial stimulation of body chemicals, the lack of control over our carnal natures, emotional or spiritual deficits in backgrounds, and weaknesses given to us by the Lord are factors that combine to create a powerful volcanic force that can literally be used by the adversary to overpower a person's ability to have control over his life and choose righteousness.

Since a transgressor, in attempting to overcome sin, is

fighting these powerful forces, no wonder it is only with the Savior, who is "mighty to save," (D&C 133:47) that one can overcome this powerful addiction and become clean and pure again. No one—*absolutely no one*—will be able to walk this path and heal without the Savior's saving strength, His redeeming power and His day-by-day guidance through the Holy Spirit.

3

The Phantom Mistress

Pornography truly can be termed "The Phantom Mistress" for a valid, justifiable reason. Participation in pornography is like bringing a mistress into the home, though this "mistress" is a distorted fantasy of machine-like, perfect-in-form-and-body creatures that a real woman could never compete against. When a transgressor views pornography and has lustful desires for other women, those women—the objects of his desire—are automatically brought into the intimate relationship between a husband and wife. This could be termed the adultery of the heart the Savior speaks so powerfully against. "Whosoever looketh on a woman, to lust after her, hath committed adultery already in his heart," He tells us. (3rd Nephi 12:28) He also says, "If thine eye be evil, thy whole body shall be full of darkness." (3rd Nephi 13:23)

Following exposure to pornography, intimacy with a wife, then—instead of being a giving, bonding act as the Lord intended—becomes a selfish act on the part of the transgressor, who is acting out his fantasy and fulfilling his lustful desires for other women. This is not true bonding or sharing but a highly damaging, destructive and degrading act—one worthy of confession.

Transgressors easily become enslaved to these "mistresses," these photo-enhanced, plastic, silicon versions of women because: 1) They are perfect in form and body; they have no flaws. They never smell; they never sweat; they never have any problems. Their beautiful bodies excite powerful emotions that thrill and stimulate—emotions that are pleasurable and addictive. These feelings offer an enticing escape to hard realities. 2) With these women, there is no commitment needed to maintain the relationship. Men are in total control of this fantasy. They desire and have an innate need for this control and power, since many other aspects of their lives do not give them this sense of control. 3) These women don't fight or have negative or hurtful feelings like wives do. They don't have any expectations that are hard to fulfill; they make no stressful demands for providing, parenting, or other responsibilities. These women provide an "out" to responsibilities transgressors don't want to face. 4) Relationships with these women create an aura of secrecy and excitement in the transgressor's life. The transgressor is essentially "living on the edge," participating in something thrilling and dangerous. These addictive emotions make him feel that he is not a failure—or, that if he is a failure outside of this, at least he can escape the reality of his failings temporarily.

> For of this sort are they which creep into houses, and lead captive silly women laden with sins, led away with divers lusts.
> . . .Do these also resist the truth: men of corrupt minds, reprobate concerning the faith. (2nd Timothy 3:6, 8)

As any form of infidelity or adultery can ruin a marriage relationship, so can pornography—which can be seen as "mental" adultery or infidelity. Pornography alone, whether or not other sexual sins accompany it, can be damaging enough to destroy the partnership between a husband and wife. Steven A. Cramer describes pornography this way:

> As pornography rots away the conscience and readies us for other sins, it also destroys our relationships with loved ones and with God. Just as the radiation from an atomic blast spreads outward, the effects of pornography also radiate outward from the center of the user into the lives of family and friends, leaving marriage and family relationships empty and hollow, stripped of the love, warmth and intimacy God meant them to have. A person addicted to pornography cannot sustain meaningful relationships because his capacity for love has been destroyed, burned away by the flames of lust, leaving him hollow and empty inside. He is incapable of giving love to others while his thoughts are constantly dominated by a gnawing hunger for the illusionary fulfillment that pornography promises but never delivers. (*Putting on the Armor of God*, p. 129)

Signs of Pornography Addiction

Men in general are usually visually oriented, noticing far more sexual things than a woman could ever fathom. It is not uncommon for a man to notice beauty of form and feature in a woman. When the carnal states take over in this process, however—when the looking tends toward lustful thoughts of action or indulgence, this is where the trouble begins. Uncontrolled thoughts, not tempered, will escalate to greater and greater sin, particularly when pornography becomes a part of this equation.

Pornography has been described as "written, graphic or other forms of communication intended to excite lascivious or lustful feelings." (*Ensign*, July 1984, p. 29) These "forms of communication" include various media such as the internet; television and movies; the phone; obscene materials such as magazines and books; or pornographic displays such as topless bars or other obscene shows.

How can we know or recognize when someone has participated in or has an addiction to pornography? The following are some guidelines and insights that might be helpful to someone working with a transgressor.

A change in personality traits. Often contention, impatience, anger, rage and an explosive temper become part of a transgressor's personality, whereas these characteristics may not have been apparent—or as apparent—before. General unhappiness, moodiness and discontent are displayed. There is also a noticeable increase of stress, anxiety and depression in a transgressor's life. Intense preoccupation and emotional distance after participation are obvious behaviors, as well.

A brooding anger and irritability exists in almost all exchanges the transgressor is involved in and comes to the forefront at the least sign of provocation. Family relationships and other associations become strained and contentious. A transgressor is easily offended or ruffled by others' behavior; he is often critical of those around him. Often those dealing with a transgressor are dumbfounded at what might cause ire or irritability.

It should be noted that if many of these negative personality traits are not unusual and have always been part of a person's life, there is a possibility that sin and transgression have always been part of that person's life, as well. "Inasmuch as thy children are conceived in sin, even so when they begin to grow up, sin conceiveth in their hearts," Moses 6:55 tells us.

Use of control and manipulation. A transgressor often becomes controlling and manipulative of his wife and children; he is quick to find fault with them, to punish or verbally chastise them, and to discipline or yell at them. He can't work through problems that have arisen but only tries to solve them by pushing them away with anger, manipulative guilt trips or blame. He often harbors resentment of past grievances and readily remembers them. Others are always to blame for these problems—never the transgressor.

Put-downs, disdain and fault-finding. There are constant put-downs by a transgressor, usually of others but sometimes of the transgressor himself. People are seen as bad, frustrating, hypocritical, false and unworthy of love and acceptance. There is growing disdain for others—in the home and outside of it—who may have been once loved and trusted. (It is interesting to note that these people often include those who would be the most instrumental in the transgressor's healing or recovery.)

Fault-finding of others increases; gossip or speaking with animosity and ill will increases; problems at work or in other areas of life escalate and become more pervasive. Other people are seen as problems, not as sources of happiness, joy and fulfillment.

Increased time away from home and family. A man engaging in pornography will begin to spend increased time away from his home and family. This man may be "out of town" for extended periods of time or have many increasing "assignments at work" which keep him away. Many times he will find or create excuses that allow him to make these escapes from home life and the demands placed on him there. These excuses may seem shallow and hollow, but when confronted about them, a transgressor will often respond with anger, irritation or blame that his motives or actions are called into question.

Evidence of half-truths, lies and deceit. There are times when family members become struck with the oddity of what seem like lies, deceit and half-truths on the part of a transgressor. When confronted about these misdeeds, a transgressor will quickly explain away his behavior or make it appear as if the person questioning his actions is the one with the problem. Just as Laman and Lemuel did to Nephi, a transgressor turns on someone questioning his integrity as being judgmental, controlling, angry, hypocritical and manipulative.

Intimacy with a wife changes. Intimacy between a husband and wife will always be affected by the use of pornography. For some transgressors, the desire for intimacy may lessen or disappear; for others, the desire for intimacy may increase and be expected—or demanded—as part of a marriage relationship. Sometimes intimacy may become one-sided (where the husband is looking for his pleasure only, not the pleasure of his wife). Or a man may lose erections or ejaculate abnormally quickly when having intercourse.

Another sign may be "weird" or "different" intimacy, intimacy that makes the wife go, "Huh?" or "Where did this come from?" Insistent demands for intimacy may often occur even when the wife is not well or has no desire for it. When there is consistent discomfort with the demands placed on a partner during intimacy, it can often be construed that there is a problem with pornography.

Usually the partner of a transgressor does not enjoy intimacy and often feels used during the process. Intimacy is rarely fulfilling and can leave a partner feeling disheartened or "yucky."

Spirituality decreases. Spirituality inevitably decreases with the use of pornography. Even if the transgressor goes to church or attempts to fulfill callings, there seems to be no real commitment or true dedication in his activity. There is usually a lackadaisical approach to all aspects of spirituality, including attempts at spirituality in the home (scripture reading, prayer, Family Night, etc.) The transgressor seldom leads out in these activities and will easily justify dismissing them. There is a noticeable lack of these in his personal life, as well.

Sometimes even anger or animosity is shown toward spiritual efforts on the part of the family or church. Religious leaders may be put down or criticized. Religious or spiritual discussions are often avoided or skirted over. Often when religious discussions come up, the transgressor cannot look the one speaking directly in the eye but seems uncomfortable with the topic. Past spiritual experiences are often brought into question or are dismissed as tainted thinking of the past.

Another extreme in relation to spirituality occurs when transgressors living a double life will tout wisdom and knowledge of gospel subjects, almost as if to cover or mask sins they know they are participating in. Or they will outwardly pretend to be involved in many righteous acts and endeavors. This helps salve consciences and gives others—and themselves—a false security about their efforts and spirituality. As it says in the Joseph Smith Translation of the *Holy Bible*, they "make [themselves] appear unto men that [they] would not commit the least sin, and yet [they, themselves] transgress the whole law." (*JST* Matthew 23:21)

A preoccupation with physical or "testosterone-building" activities. Many transgressors become obsessed with activities that build their egos, not their self-worth. A transgressor many times becomes "addicted" to these activities. Excessive indulgence in sports (for example, weight-lifting, golfing, water-skiing, cycling—motor or otherwise, hunting, running, biking, etc.) can be one indication of something amiss. Other activities might include intense preoccupation with vehicles (boats, Jeeps, motorcycles, four-wheelers, sports cars, etc.), excessive yard work, intense absorption with hobbies or other similar activities. Sometimes longer hours at work become a major part of a transgressor's life.

Inability to sit still, especially in social situations or when attempting to relax; may only sit still in front of a computer or TV. Many transgressors cannot sit still and become "antsy" when doing nothing or attempting to relax. They often cannot be around large groups of people for long and will try to escape the noise and confusion as soon as possible. The only time they may have the ability to sit still is when working with a computer or watching TV. Sometimes they feel an intense need to get away and do something or they feel as if they'll go "crazy."

Often engages in "mind-numbing" or "mind-dulling"

behaviors. Transgressors often adopt behaviors to dull or numb the mind, especially during times of discouragement or depression. These activities may include anything that lets them escape from the realities of family life or interacting with people. (This usually causes resentment or discouragement in those dealing with them when they cannot effectively pull them away from these behaviors.)

Activities may include such things as eating as a way of escape, frequently playing video or computer games, "channel surfing" while watching TV or frequently surfing the internet, excessive movie or TV watching, reading unbalanced amounts of light reading in comparison to other "deeper" reading, absorption with hobbies, etc. These behaviors are often chosen over alternative activities, especially interacting with others.

It should be noted here that many mind-numbing and mind-dulling behaviors can be deep-seated and may have been a precursor to addictive behaviors, not just a consequence of them.

Changes in physical appearance or habits. With the use of pornography, there are usually noticeable changes in the physical habits or appearance of the transgressor. There may be an increased preoccupation with the physical aspect of one's life or a transgressor may let his physical state slide. These changes become noticeable in such things as clothing, hair, weight or other lifestyle changes. Some become slothful and lazy (there is a depressing spirit about them); some become intensely conscious about their physical appearance, spending a lot of time and money on themselves.

Lack of ability to sleep at night. A transgressor will often struggle with an increased lack of ability to sleep, even when he is home. He is usually up late and keeps odd hours and patterns. He may blame these patterns on work or other physical problems.

Cyclical ups and downs in a marriage and other relationships. There may be times when a transgressor seems fine—when he is kind, attentive to the family, and patient with home life and children. Other aspects of his life seem to smooth out, as well. These "honeymoon" periods will always be followed by a relapse into old patterns of anger, contention, impatience, blame, discouragement, depression and anxiety—similar to a Dr. Jekyll/Mr. Hyde compartmentalizing of the personality.

Those dealing with a transgressor often look on in consternation at the fall downward, wondering what could possibly bring about these awful changes when everything seemed to be "fine and okay." They become baffled by their own perceptions of reality and sometimes wonder, after the honeymoon periods, "Was I only dreaming things were okay? How did we get to this awful point so easily?"

Emotional distance and "glazed" eyes. After participation in pornography, there will often be emotional distance and "glazed" eyes—a glassy, distant stare that is noticeable. It may be hard for a transgressor to concentrate and interact, especially with eye to eye contact during discussions. Usually isolation is sought shortly thereafter. Sometimes, however, intimacy or a "release" is sought—or demanded—from a wife.

A noticeable change in the spirit of the home, whether or not the transgressor is present. Many times close family members of a transgressor can actually feel or sense when that person has committed a pornographic act—even if that transgressor is not present in the home at the time of participation. There is a noticeable change in the atmosphere and spirit of the home—from "okay" or peaceful to dark, gloomy, evil, depressing and heavy. Often innocent parties feeling this change of spirit become troubled, agitated, sad, overwhelmed, miserable or discouraged. They usually have no idea where these feelings come from and don't know how to fight or push them away—despite the desire to do so.

Swearing or other changes in language. Often a transgressor will adopt rude or foul language or will swear more consistently. Standards previously held may be relaxed or discarded.

Noticeably looser standards with movies, music and books. Many transgressors, who might have been vigilant and rigid before about what was brought into a home, become more relaxed with standards of entertainment. When a wife or others question his behavior or choices, it is shrugged off as inconsequential, bothersome, controlling or overbearing.

Looks lustfully at women in every-day interaction; treats women as subservient or inferior. Many transgressors begin looking at women differently, even in normal, every-day interactions. "Lingering" eyes on women is one way lust is manifest. Some women may sense the openness of a transgressor and "hit upon them" or make moves toward a relationship involving intimacy.

Treating women as subservient or inferior is another behavior that often accompanies transgression. Usually there is control, manipulation, blame or irritation that accompanies requests from a transgressor for a woman to perform tasks or during other interaction.

Unexplained increases in expenditures. A transgressor participating in pornography will usually have an increased cash outlay or increases in credit card bills. Watch for increasing expenses in things such as charges for internet sites, phone bills, or unknown expenses on credit cards. Unexplained cash withdrawals may also escalate. Many do not manage money well in other aspects of their lives.

Denies or trivializes a problem with pornography. All transgressors addicted to pornography—even if a problem is out in the open—do not see their participation as a problem but as trivial, inconsequential, isolated incidents that can be easily minimized and glossed over. (For example, one man did not see walking into a topless bar during his "recovery phase" as a problem since he didn't stay long; he was only "toying" with the idea of participating.)

In the transgressor's mind, then, "all men do this." There exists an inability to own up to a problem or see the problem with the severity in which it needs to be seen.

As shown from the above examples, even when a transgressor cannot admit to a problem with pornography in his life, there are many outside indications that there is something amiss. "Ye shall know them by their fruits," the scriptures tell us. "Do men gather grapes of thorns, or figs of thistles? Even so every good tree bringeth forth good fruit; but a corrupt tree bringeth forth evil fruit. . . .Wherefore, by their fruits ye shall know them." (3 Nephi 14:16-17, 20) Also,

> . . .A bitter fountain cannot bring forth good water; neither can a good fountain bring forth bitter water; wherefore, a man being a servant of the devil cannot follow Christ; and if he follow Christ he cannot be a servant of the devil.
> . . .All things which are good cometh of God; and that which is evil cometh of the devil; for the devil is an enemy unto God, and fighteth against him continually, and inviteth and enticeth to sin, and to do that which is evil continually. (Moroni 7: 11-12)

Getting to "Yes"

In order to move forward toward any type of healing, a transgressor must begin to see and admit to a problem with pornography. Dr. Lynn Scoresby, a prominent family counselor who understands and has worked in great depth with pornography addictions, said during one group presentation that cyclical patterns often accompany the behavior of pornography addicts.

In this cycle, an escalation phase begins the pattern. This phase is characterized by the beliefs or impaired thinking that lead the transgressor to participate in sin. It includes such triggers as certain times, events, mental attitudes, actions and behaviors that lead one to indulgence in pornography.

This escalation phase is then followed by the "participation phase" in which, despite all previous resolve to refrain from sin, the transgressor falls and succumbs to temptation. This fall inevitably brings guilt and shame, feelings that evoke remorse or despair. The transgressor then adopts the determination to never participate in pornography again. Because of this determination to reform his behavior, this squelches or suppresses the idea that he has a problem. Thinking such as: "This was a minor mishap; I'll just control my behaviors so I won't fall again"; "I can easily overcome this; I'll plunge myself into work, church or other activities so I am not tempted" become a part of his reasoning.

The transgressor believes in his resolution to not fall again and may, in fact, go through a brief period of self-imposed "reform." This phase can produce denial on the part of the transgressor. The transgressor literally does not believe he has a problem; though everything in his life indicates one exists, he deludes himself into thinking he won't fall and that he can—and has—easily overcome his tendencies. Little does he realize that when confronted with the same environment, thoughts, life pressures and events, his determination to refrain will crumble and he will participate in pornography once more, beginning the addictive cycle again.

This cycle may occur over and over again in the life of a transgressor, becoming deeper and more pervasive—and often leading a transgressor to even more serious sin. As the scriptures say, "Evil men and seducers shall wax worse and worse, deceiving, and being deceived." (2nd Timothy 3:13) The only way to break this cycle, Dr. Scoresby claims, is by getting to "yes." The transgressor must admit, "Yes, I have a problem"; "Yes, I participate in and have an addiction to behaviors I know are wrong"; "Yes, I've told lies and deceived people in order to hide this sin"; "Yes, I need help to overcome this." Admitting these truths is an essential first step in breaking the vicious cycle of pornography addiction.

Two different scenarios occur in a transgressor getting to this point of acknowledging a problem. The first occurs when the transgressor comes forward on his own and admits to the double life of deception he's been involved in. He can no longer stand his life of sin and wants to become clean again. This is by far the best scenario in terms of healing and becoming whole for "he that truly humbleth himself, and repenteth of his sins. . .the same shall be blessed—yea, much more blessed than they who are compelled to be humble." (Alma 32:15)

The second scenario is far more difficult and arduous. Those that are "compelled to be humble" (Alma 32:14) because they are "caught" or "found out" face a much more rocky road—not only for them but for those around them. Intense denial, refusal to face up to an addiction and an unwillingness to change always occur at the outset of this scenario. Confession means losing control of the ability to hide the secretiveness and darkness of the double life they have been involved in; they would have to face up to their own lies—to themselves and others—if they do admit to a problem. They fight to keep darkness hidden with intense and insistent denial.

A wife or other close associate who confronts a transgressor will struggle intensely through this period. She will receive reactions of anger and animosity with any suggestion there is something wrong; she is often accused of overreacting. She may be blamed for being judgmental, unforgiving, untrusting and hypocritical. Past behaviors or problems of her own may be criticized and used to justify the current behavior of the transgressor.

Often during this period actual proof or further evidence is needed to bring the transgressor to a point of admitting a problem. One woman, for example, in getting her husband to admit to his pornography addiction, actually had to go to a video store and re-rent all of the movies that were on her husband's history list. She got these movies and set them on the counter in her home before she confronted her husband about his behavior. This was the first time he admitted to any type of problem.

Another woman confronted her husband after finding pornographic internet sites on his computer. After first trying to explain away the appearance of the sites, only then did he admit to having a problem with pornography—which, even then, was only "slight." In another instance, one woman noticed something wrong when she found unknown expenses on their credit card bills. When she finally traced these expenses, she found out many of them were phone cards used for her husband's problem.

Because of the initial reactions of denial by transgressors, some women sincerely wonder if they are "making a big deal out of nothing" or are skewed in their own thinking and judgment regarding their situations. Their husbands may seem sincere in their lies and justification; they've had no reason to distrust their husbands before, have they? Shouldn't they believe their claims of guiltlessness now?

These women need to come to trust themselves when they sense inwardly, "Something is wrong; this doesn't feel right." With this knowledge, powerful and pleading prayers may ascend to the Lord that He will "discover unto my people who serve me. . .the works of their brethren, yea, their secret works, their works of darkness, and their wickedness and abominations. . . .I will bring forth out of darkness unto light all their secret works and their abominations." (Alma 37:23, 25) The Lord can and will help "hidden things of darkness" (D&C 123:13) come to light so that these women are not destroyed by the darkness that pervades everything around them because of the unrighteous choices of others.

Truly, the very first step on the long road to recovery for a pornography addict is getting to "yes"—admitting that there is a problem, admitting the depth of the problem and admitting that help is needed in overcoming the problem. As the scriptures say, "light and truth forsake the evil one." (D&C 93:37) "Therefore, . . .we should waste and wear out our lives in bringing to light all the hidden things of darkness, wherein we know them; and they are truly manifest from heaven—These shall be attended to with great earnestness." (D&C 123:13-14) This one step is the essential beginning on the long road to recovery and healing, for the Lord "will not spare them" if they continue to "pollute their inheritances." (D&C 103:14)

> And now, my brethren, I wish from the inmost part of my heart, yea, with great anxiety even unto pain, that ye would hearken unto my words, and cast off your sins, and not procrastinate the day of your repentance;
> But that ye would humble yourselves before the Lord, and call upon his holy name, and watch and pray continually, that ye may not be tempted above that which ye can bear. (Alma 13:27-28)

> Verily, verily I say unto you, darkness covereth the earth, and gross darkness the minds of the people, and all flesh has become corrupt before my face.
> Behold, vengeance cometh speedily upon the face of the earth, a day of wrath, a day of burning, a day of desolation, of weeping, of mourning, and of lamentation; and as a whirlwind it shall come upon all the face of the earth, saith the Lord.
> And upon my house shall it begin, and from my house shall it go forth, saith the Lord;
> First among those among you, saith the Lord, who have professed to know my name and have not known me, and have blasphemed against me in the midst of my house, saith the Lord. (D&C 112:23-26)

> Wherefore, prepare ye, prepare ye, O my people; sanctify yourselves;
> . . .Go ye out from Babylon. Be ye clean that bear the vessels of the Lord. (D&C 133:4-5)

4

Confession: A Crucial Step

Bruce R. McConkie, in *Mormon Doctrine*, quoted the following statement:

> "We desire with holy zeal to emphasize the enormity of sexual sins," President Joseph F. Smith has said. "Though often regarded as insignificant by those not knowing the will of God, they are in his eyes an abomination; and if we are to remain his favored people, they must be shunned as the gates of hell. The evil results of these sins are so patent in vice, crime, misery and disease that it would appear that all, young and old, must perceive and sense them. They are destroying the world. If we are to be preserved we must abhor them, shun them, not practice the least of them, for they weaken and enervate, they kill man spiritually, they make him unfit for the company of the righteous and the presence of God." (Gospel Doctrine, 5th ed., pp. 275-276) (p. 709)

Because pornography is such an abominable sin, confession by the transgressor is an essential, imperative step on the road to recovery and healing. If confession does not occur, then healing becomes *impossible* for a transgressor. The poison of this darkness and evil will always be in his life—and grow stronger and more uncontrollable—until the light of the Savior pierces it and eliminates it. The Savior's light first shines on a soul thus darkened with the necessary first step of confession.

We submit that not only priesthood leaders—Bishops or Stake Presidents—need to hear a full confession of sin, but also the wives of a transgressor *must* become a part of this confession. The reasoning for confessing to a wife is twofold. First of all, when a marriage occurs, a covenant relationship is made in a triangular pattern between the Savior, the husband and the wife. When the covenant relationship is broken between the wife and the husband because of transgression, the wife has the right and indeed must know the transgression *in this life* in order to heal this broken covenant relationship.

If the husband's deeds are not known here, *they will be made known later*. This is a truthful fact. The Lord has told us in the scriptures that, during the millennial reign, "There is nothing which is secret save it shall be revealed; there is no work of darkness save it shall be made manifest in the light." (2 Nephi 30:17) He also states, "All things shall be revealed unto the children of men which ever have been among the children of men, and which ever will be even unto the end of the earth." (2 Nephi 27:11) He warns us that "the rebellious shall be pierced with much sorrow; for their iniquities shall be spoken upon the housetops, and their secret acts shall be revealed." (D&C 1:3)

As the Prophet Joseph Smith said, "Our acts are recorded, and at a future day they will be laid before us, and if we should fail to judge right and injure our fellow-beings, they may there, perhaps condemn us; *there they are of great consequence, and to me the consequence appears to be of force, beyond anything which I am able to express." (Teachings of the Prophet Joseph Smith,* p. 69, italics added)

Vaughn J. Featherstone stated it this way:

> Picture a huge scroll sliding down from the ceiling. On it are listed the names of those who purchased pornographic literature. The list is large enough so that all may see. Is your name on the list? Now suppose those names are removed, and the names of all those who attended or viewed X-rated movies are presented so that all who are in the congregation may see. Again, is your name on the list?
>
> . . .How about all those who have a masturbation problem? . . .What if we had the names of those who had a homosexual problem. . .then we had those who are adulterers, who are serving in priesthood positions, unbeknownst to many, unbeknownst unto anyone except themselves and the partner in sin?
>
> . . .I bear my solemn witness that *if you do not self-inflict a purging in your lives, the time may well come when there might not be a scroll, but it will be as though there were. It may be as though it had been shouted from the tops of the houses. People cannot hide sin. You cannot mock God and hold the Lord's holy priesthood and pretend that you are his servant.* (*Ensign,* May 1975, p. 66, italics added)

Confession of sins to both the wife and the appropriate priesthood holders is an essential part of purging. If those sins are confessed and healed in this life, then, as the Lord has said, "He who has repented of his sins, the same is forgiven, and I, the Lord, *remember them no more.* By this ye may know if a man repenteth of his sins—behold, he will *confess them* and forsake them." (D&C 58:42-43, italics added)

There is a second reason a transgressor should confess to a wife. As one Bishop said, when a transgressor only confesses to the priesthood authority over him and not to his partner, this is like two men "colluding" against the wife. It is unfair and unjust to the one truly injured and betrayed by the sin. It is not only the covenant with the Savior that has been broken by the transgression, but also the covenant with the wife. She has a right and a responsibility to know when this has happened. As President Kimball has said in *The Miracle of Forgiveness*, "When one has wronged another in deep transgression. . .he, the aggressor, who gave the offense. . .should immediately make amends by confessing to the injured one and doing all in his power to clear up the matter." (p. 186)

Serious spiritual danger also results from not confessing to a wife. The transgressor often feels safe from accountability. This opens him up to incomplete healing and the possibility of future sin. What does he have to lose if he sins again when his wife will always be unaware of what is happening? Is there any risk involved if his partner never knows his actions?

Unless there is complete, total confession to the proper priesthood authorities and a wife, true healing *will not* follow. In many, many cases where there has been a pornography addiction and confession only occurred to the Bishop, recurrences of the problem transpired later. This "recurrence" happens with increased darkness, trauma and devastation since "unto that soul who sinneth shall the former sins return." (D&C 82:7) It is as if dealing with everything one dealt with previously with the added sins of the new transgressions. It is imperative that one confesses to a wife in order to break this cycle.

One Bishop counseled a transgressor, in essence: "Tell your wife everything; hold nothing back. Let her question and re-question you as needed about past events. She is the one who has been violated; it is not only your covenant with the Savior but your covenant relationship with her that has been destroyed. She has a right to know whatever she feels she needs to know regarding these sins."

As the Prophet Joseph Smith said, "Let. . .all the Saints be willing to confess all their sins, and not keep back a part."

(*Teachings*, p. 155) We have seen that in all relationships where there has been healing after a betrayal with pornography or other sexual sins, there have been honest, complete and open confessions to not only the priesthood authorities but to the wives of those transgressors. When confessions have not occurred, the sinning parties most often move on to deeper and deeper transgression, destroying many marriages and relationships completely.

Because of this, it is no wonder that Satan does not want sinning parties to confess to a wife. He knows deep, inward healing can begin to occur only when this happens. Unless they are counseled to do so, however, transgressors will rarely take this step and will often try to keep their transgressions hidden from a partner. As one transgressor said angrily to a wife who had confronted him about not being a part of his confession, "Why have you suddenly become my Bishop? I've confessed to him. Why do I have to confess to you? Do you think you're my judge now? Isn't it enough to come clean with the Bishop?" It was uncovered shortly after this statement that his confession to the Bishop had not been complete and had been glossed over by half-truths. There still existed after this attempted confession deep, continuing sins that left the problems of contention and bickering resurfacing in their marriage. After the wife expressed her concerns to their Bishop and he chose to confront the transgressor again, only then did the full truth come out. The deeper sins were uncovered and exposed at that time.

Truly, the cycle of healing can only begin once a transgressor confesses completely to a Bishop and his wife. A wife can then become an instrumental part in the healing process instead of being an outsider watching something she has no control over.

A strenuous warning needs to be inserted at this point. *When there are not complete, honest, and open confessions by a transgressor—that is, if a transgressor continues to lie, paint half-truths or gloss over sins of the past, the pain, devastation, turmoil and agony of the partner hearing confessions will occur over and over and over again. This will not stop until sufficient and honest confessions are made.* Despite how ugly, painful and difficult it is to hear undiluted truth, it is an absolutely necessary step in order to move forward toward healing.

The Lord will truly bless the one hearing a confession to know when sufficient truth is out. A peaceful confirmation will occur. When one does not have this peace of mind, it can be construed that there are continuing lies, half-truths or glossing of sins. A transgressor's kindest act, as difficult as it may sound, is getting everything out in the open so healing may begin.

It also should be taken into account that once adequate confession to a wife occurs, the unnecessary re-hashing of past events needs to come to a stop. Delving too deeply and too often into past sins can become severely damaging for both the transgressor and his partner. The haunting thoughts and ideas planted by Satan in the mind of an innocent party need to be fought as fiercely and unremittingly as the damaging thoughts he places in the mind of a transgressor. We still assert with absolute conviction that a wife should hear the confession. Nevertheless, if this is not done with the proper balance of "letting go of the past" when necessary, it can become damaging and destructive instead of becoming healing.

When Transgressors Won't Admit to a Problem with Pornography Despite Telling Evidence That One Exists

Since getting to "yes" is such an essential part of the healing process, *there will be no movement toward healing until this occurs with a transgressor.* Yet so often denial is so ingrained and innate in a transgressor's life that even glimmers of direct evidence will not cause a transgressor to admit to the actual truth. (For example, one man found with a pornographic magazine in his room claimed he had "taken it away from a friend to keep him from viewing it." Another man who had been caught with pornographic sites on his internet claimed they had just been sent automatically; "everyone gets them.")

It is hard, devastating and emotionally wearing to a

wife or other person working with this kind of transgressor. This transgressor has truly become "hardened and impenitent." (Alma 47:36) He has no desire to repent or change, or he completely lacks the ability to see or acknowledge he has a problem.

Many times people working with these transgressors are overwhelmed and even frightened when facing the hardship of having the sole responsibility of bringing darkness into the light so healing can begin. This concept of being frightened and overwhelmed can be illustrated by the true story of a woman who was intensely scared of an underground cellar in her home where she grew up. She hated this dark, musty cellar; she never dared go inside, not knowing what evils or dangers lurked therein. She harbored this intense fear even as a mother with children of her own.

One day the threat of a tornado caused this woman to have to take her children and approach the cellar. Despite knowing her desperate need to get inside this cellar, her overwhelming fears arose and she said in pleading prayer, "Oh Father, I'm so scared to go inside the cellar."

The Father's answering impression came immediately into her mind. He said, "Then do it scared." In other words, despite her terrible fears and the uncertainty she felt, she still had to go inside and face the darkness she had feared her whole life because of the intense need to do so for her safety and the safety of her children.

This situation is similar to those working with unrepentant transgressors. Facing the path ahead and knowing they are the ones that must bring out the truth is dark, ominous and frightening. These partners truly feel alone and vulnerable when facing these awful realities. But in order for any progress at all to occur, one must "do it scared"—go down this path no matter how ugly, intimidating or frightening it may be. True spiritual safety lies in this step. If this is not done, a transgressor will continue to move further and further downward in a spiraling cycle of sin, hurting himself and others even more terribly.

The first thing one must do in getting the truth out is to hold on to the surety and certainty that *there is a problem* when one senses innately or spiritually that there is. It can be incredibly difficult, arduous and wearing to hold on to this truth. A transgressor has become an instrument of Satan in manipulation, deceit and control; he will often use anger or guilt as tools to inflict venom on the person confronting him. He inevitably turns against this person as the one with the problem. That party is often accused of being judgmental, emotionally unstable, overreactive, a troublemaker, contentious, manipulative, untrusting and unkind. Often these barbs are flung so frequently and so often that the person confronting a transgressor reels with pain and injury at the incessant attacks that come. Doubts and confusion may surface; self-doubt may occur.

Other times a transgressor may become extra "spiritual," seemingly humble, kind, sensitive and caring of a partner at these times in order to gloss over his problems, hoping a wife will see from his sensitivity and kindness that there is no possible way he has a problem. Positive traits and behaviors will be touted in an effort to prove worthiness. This approach throws a wife off even further in her suspicions. For one thing, a husband truly believes he has been reformed. He honestly thinks he will continue to live righteously. Negative behaviors, however, will always resurface, usually within a fairly short period of time.

Through prayer and intense pleading, a person confronting a transgressor who is in denial may rest assured that the Lord's "wisdom is greater than the cunning of the devil" (D&C 10:43), that they are right in their suspicions of guilt, and that the Lord will make all things known in His "own due time." (Mormon 5:12)

> Behold, I, the Lord, have looked upon you,
> and have seen abominations in the church that

profess my name.

. . .Wo unto them that are deceivers and hypocrites, for, thus saith the Lord, I will bring them to judgment.

. . .There are hypocrites among you, who have deceived some, which has given the adversary power; but behold, such shall be reclaimed;

But the hypocrites shall be detected and shall be cut off, either in life or in death, even as I will;

. . .Wherefore, let every man beware lest he do that which is not in truth and righteousness before me. (D&C 50:4, 6-9)

There were among you adulterers and adulteresses; some of whom have turned away from you, and others remain with you that hereafter shall be revealed.

Let such beware and repent speedily, lest judgment shall come upon them as a snare, and their folly shall be made manifest, and their works shall follow them in the eyes of the people. (D&C 63:14-15)

Ye cannot hide your crimes from God; and except ye repent they will stand as a testimony against you at the last day.

. . .Ye should repent and forsake your sins, and go no more after the lusts of your eyes, but cross yourself in all these things; for except ye do this ye can in nowise inherit the kingdom of God. (Alma 39:8-9)

Satan knows that once darkness is unearthed, he begins losing control over a transgressor. That is why often the intensity of darkness and evil emotion from a transgressor seem to escalate when one is attempting to get the truth out. In fact, the closer one gets to discovering the truth, the greater and more intense become the onslaughts from the adversary. Anger erupts at the slightest provocation; intense and bitter confrontations follow without the ability to work through issues; resentments and past grievances are openly expressed; separation and divorce are often threatened. Feelings of darkness and evil inside the home seem to increase and become heavy, even when the transgressor is not present. All these are indications of Satan fighting to hold on to his grip around a transgressor.

There are righteous forces a person may garner, however, when trying to get the truth out. The first and most essential force includes righteous priesthood holders who can help and counsel both the transgressor and the person confronting him. The Bishop should ideally be foremost in this battle. Deep concerns about the actions and behavior of a transgressor must be shared and even feelings or spiritual promptings expressed. A Bishop is a "judge in Israel" who will often "judge his people by the testimony of the just." (D&C 58: 17-18) He can many times confront a transgressor and, with the mantle of discernment given to him by Heavenly Father, come to learn the truth. He can then help a transgressor begin to let go of denial and admit to his problems—thus beginning the road to healing.

Sometimes seeking professional counselors or guidance from others who have transgressed may be effective as well, particularly if these people have worked extensively with those dealing with pornography or other addictions. Even if the transgressor is not willing to seek this kind of counseling, the wife or other party can learn necessary skills and develop understanding about the behavioral traits, actions and attitudes of a transgressor. With this ammunition, a partner can continue to assert that a problem exists until it surfaces in either discovery or confession.

Often "discovery"—or finding hard evidence to show one knows a transgressor is involved in sin—is an essential step in moving a transgressor toward confession. This can be scary and frightening to one already dealing with the confusion, heartache and suffering that comes when questioning the integrity of a marriage and a partner. This task becomes overwhelming because a partner must look for signs—actual evidence of participation—in such things as private records, movie rentals, internet sites, stashes of magazines or other obscene materials, evidence of cash withdrawals or credit card expenses, etc. This can make someone feel sneaky, suspicious, untrustworthy and uncertain of one's own personal actions.

One woman shared her experience as she went through the difficulty of knowing she had to find proof to bring out her husband's sins. She had caught him some time earlier with pornographic internet sites on his computer, but he had claimed to have confessed to his Bishop and cleared up the problem. His behaviors and attitudes—and the continual contention in the marriage—made this woman believe a problem still existed. Prayer confirmed her suspicions. Every time she confronted her husband about her beliefs, however, he vehemently denied any involvement in pornography. He got so angry at her accusations and suspicions that he actually threatened to divorce her, saying she was the one off base, that she was emotionally unstable and that he had grown tired of having to deal with her anger and distrust. Why did he have to live with someone as vindictive and vengeful as she had become? he would ask her. Hadn't he taken care of his problems in the appropriate way? Did she expect more? Would she always hang his past over his head and keep throwing it in his face when he had done everything he needed to do to rectify it?

This woman came to realize the only way she would get her husband to confess to sinning consisted in actually finding proof of his participation. She had an extremely difficult time knowing she needed to become a "detective" and secretively search out her husband's actions. She had always been completely open and honest with him in all aspects of their relationship; she almost felt as if she was sinning against her covenants and bringing into question her own integrity by being deceptive and secretive and "going behind his back" to do this.

She struggled with this intense inner conflict of emotion during the darkness of one painful night, knowing she needed to somehow move forward but feeling as if she had chosen to actually fight and turn against her own husband. As she agonized over her situation, a powerful impression came into her mind from the Lord. "You are not fighting against your husband," the Lord clearly told her. "You are fighting against Satan." Simultaneously with this impression she felt as if spiritual armor had literally been placed around her. She felt an endowment of the inner strength and fortitude she needed to begin the difficult task of exposing her husband's problem. She knew, most importantly, that it needed to be done in order for any type of healing to occur.

After counseling with some people familiar with pornography addictions, she decided to secretively search the history on her husband's computer—even the cookie files that had been purposefully erased by him. (See the "Appendix" in this book for information regarding the internet site that can do this.) She found a history of pornographic sites, some as early as two weeks before. Because of this, she could then take this information to both her husband and their Bishop. After being confronted, her husband finally admitted the truth of his continuing addiction. The road to healing had finally begun. "Then shall ye return and discern between the righteous and the wicked, between him that serveth God and him that serveth him not," the scriptures tell us. (3rd Nephi 24:18)

Many women, in questioning transgressors' behavior, have a hard time becoming "investigators." They can hardly stand to face the truth that their husbands do indeed have a problem with pornography; it sickens, disgusts and disheartens them that this ugly reality could be occurring in their marriages and lives. Denial often becomes a common escape route for them, too, and they often avoid or gloss over issues, pretending—or believing their husbands' words—that there is nothing wrong.

As hard as it is to confront and face truth about pornography addiction, *it must be done.* A transgressor who does not confess on his own will always go into deeper and deeper sin. The only way to stop this cycle is by bringing about a confession of truth. As one woman stated, she had to "dig and dig until the truth came out. I knew I would never get to the bottom of it all unless I did confront my husband harshly like I did. I kept pushing and pushing him, making him reveal more—even though he kept telling me that I was 'distrusting' and that this was my problem, not his. As he continued to turn on me in anger, this became more evidence to me that there was something further he was hiding."

She continues, "I had to always think it was worse than what I'd heard so I would keep questioning him until the full truth came out. The Lord helped me during this time to keep me pushing like I did. He whispered to me, 'You've got to get all of the roots out or you'll never kill the weed.' This sustained me to keep prying until I knew the truth was sufficient. Once it was, I fell into a crumpled heap of emotion." As hard as this experience was for her, it was the turning point in the healing of her marriage.

Women truly become the vessels by which marriages are cleansed, but this only happens when truth is disclosed. Many women often have to become the instruments by which hard and ugly realities come to the fore. This is not an easy part of the repentance process, but it is absolutely necessary for any type of healing to begin.

The Lord will many times give insights and sustaining strength to women to help them through this difficult time of uncovering truth. He will often whisper thoughts and direction in moving forward during these times. A woman must trust and know she will not be alone in this but will have the Lord by her side to help her in this "discovery" process.

One woman's experience illustrates this. This woman, Trisa* (*names have been changed) saw evidence of the darkness of participation in the countenance of one of her brothers-in-law, Sam. (Trisa could recognize this darkness because of having gone through a similar situation with her own husband.) When Trisa told her sister what she had witnessed in Sam, her sister immediately went home and confronted him. He vehemently denied any involvement. Because of this, this sister began doubting the impression regarding him, saying Trisa had been wrong.

Trisa, not doubting in the least her impressions, had the further inspiration to call Sam directly. In the course of the conversation, in asking about what he had done during the time her sister had recently been away on a trip, she felt inspired of the Lord to ask him, "What kind of movies did you watch while she was gone, Sam?"

Her question was met with dead silence. Sam quickly made an excuse and hung up the phone, needing to go on home teaching visits. Her sister immediately called back after Sam had left, wanting to know what Trisa had said to him. "He was as pale as a ghost and broke out in a sweat," her sister explained. "His countenance completely changed. What did you say? It struck him straight in the heart."

When Trisa told her what she had asked, her sister quickly acknowledged, "He did watch bad movies, didn't he." His reaction had been enough evidence to her that he had become involved in pornography. That night, when Sam came home from home teaching, his wife confronted him again about pornography. Once more, any participation was vehemently denied. A second and third time she confronted him, and again he denied any participation.

She spent a sleepless night beside her husband, awoke and then confronted him one more time. "I couldn't sleep at all," she told him. "I feel I'm troubled for a reason. Did you watch bad movies while I was gone on my trip?"

"No, I didn't," Sam insisted. "I'm not lying."

She became certain he had, however, and knowing it had been movies that had become his downfall, she went to places where he might have rented them. She got his "history" from store personnel and re-rented several that she came to find out were indeed pornographic. She took these home and set them on the counter.

Once again, when Sam came home, she confronted him about his behavior. "Did you watch any pornographic movies while I was gone?" she asked him.

Again, the denial. "No, I did not."

"You're a liar," she said. She showed him the movies she had found from his history list. Only then did Sam admit to the truth and the long journey of their healing began.

The Lord has told us: "Behold, I say unto you that whoso believeth in Christ, doubting nothing, whatsoever he shall ask the Father in the name of Christ it shall be granted him; and this promise is unto all, even unto the ends of the earth." (Mormon 9:21)

> Therefore, verily I say unto you, lift up your voices unto this people; speak the thoughts that I shall put into your hearts, and you shall not be confounded before me;
>
> For it shall be given you in the very hour, yea, in the very moment, what ye shall say.
>
> But a commandment I give unto you, that ye shall declare whatsoever thing ye declare in my name, in solemnity of heart, in the spirit of meekness, in all things.
>
> And I give unto you this promise, that inasmuch as ye do this the Holy Ghost shall be shed forth in bearing record unto all things whatsoever ye shall say.
>
> . . .Therefore, continue your journey and let your hearts rejoice; for behold, and lo, I am with you even unto the end. (D&C 100:5-8, 12)

Truth Comes Out "Line Upon Line, Precept Upon

Precept" (D&C 128:21)

Even if a transgressor gets to the point where he begins to confess his sins, it needs to be noted that the complete truth will never come out all at once. Never. This circumstance occurs for several reasons. First and foremost, when a transgressor has been involved in sin, there are often pockets of deeper sins buried beneath layers of other sins more readily remembered. As each layer of sin is confessed, more and more of the deeply buried sins will be exposed and will come to the surface.

This can be illustrated by an experience in the life of Steven A. Cramer in *The Worth of a Soul*. Though he had confessed to the proper priesthood authorities and his wife, he took each of his sins, one by one, and confessed them to the Lord.

> Starting with my worst sins, the adultery, the pornography, the self-stimulation, I began confessing. I verbally identified and described every deliberate sin I could remember and surrendered each of them, asking [the Lord] to apply the Savior's atonement to free me from them.
>
> . . .This wonderful process is part of what it took to break the pride and stubbornness in my heart and make my spirit more contrite, soft, and yielding to the Spirit.
>
> This experience was so real to me that it was almost tangible. I could actually feel myself being cleansed. . .It was so real to me that it almost seemed as if I were kneeling at the feet of my Heavenly Father and my Savior, and They were saying to me, "We have been waiting such a long time for you to share these burdens with Us. We are so glad that at last you have decided to believe Us and to trust Us and to come to Us so that We may do for you all that We have promised to do for each man's salvation."
>
> What I have described was a process, not a single event. I had to go through these surrendering

sessions for several months *as other sins came to mind which I had forgotten.* Each bit of poison thusly surrendered made my load lighter and increased my love for Heavenly Father and the Savior. (pp. 99-100, italics added)

This exposing of deeper pockets of sin can also be illustrated allegorically by the experience of one woman who took her son in to have infection surgically removed from his ear. After the surgeon had gone in and removed the infection that had shown in the x-rays that had been taken, there was a deeper pocket of infection hidden directly beneath it. This infection had been in the ear for so long it had actually hardened and rotted away part of the essential ear apparatus, including the eardrum, causing irreparable damage. It took hours to cleanse this and major reconstructive surgery would have to ensue. This poisonous pocket was hidden beneath the superficial infection that showed initially, much like deeper sins hidden below the more external ones of a transgressor.

Another reason that truth never comes out all at once exists in the fact that transgressors have literally been involved in lies and deception for so long that, like Korihor in the *Book of Mormon*, they are "possessed with a lying spirit." (Alma 30:42) Some have told these lies for so long that they "verily believ(e) that they [are] true." (Alma 30:53) Starting to confess, then, and beginning to tell the truth, is, as one woman was told in a counseling session, a "process of moving from the telestial to the celestial." *It will not happen all at once.* Just as it took time to fall and transgress, so does it take time to heal. Transgressors are almost re-learning what truth is, how to tell the complete truth, and how to differentiate truth from the deception of the double lives they have been leading. This is a process of time and effort. As more and more light comes into a transgressor's life, more and more truth will come to the fore.

A third reason transgressors never admit the complete truth initially lies in the fact that they can never clearly see the seriousness of their sins at the start of the repentance process.

Once they have been involved in transgression, as the scriptures say, "He that looketh on a woman to lust after her, or if any shall commit adultery in their hearts, *they shall not have the Spirit.*" (D&C 63:16, italics added) With the loss of the spirit, thinking becomes skewed and ideas are tainted by the adversary's forces of darkness and evil. The adversary convinces transgressors that their sins are minor. These sins are seen as inconsequential and insignificant errors, only involving or affecting themselves—a tiny glitch in their lives that can easily be glossed over or dismissed. Anger, contention, manipulation, blame and control have become part of their personalities and behaviors, but they see nothing wrong with these and see everyone outside themselves as the problem. These are examples of a few effects of the loss of the spirit, but many other negative attitudes and behaviors are adopted, as well.

As transgressors embrace righteous principles into their lives and the cleansing process of repentance begins, they will begin to see more and more clearly the repugnant ugliness that has become a part of their souls and lives because of their transgressions. They will begin to slowly discern and dissect the darkness that has permeated their lives. They will also begin to understand more clearly the lies Satan has fed to them for as long as they have been living these double lives—lies they once thought were truths.

This idea can be illustrated by an incident involving a Colorado farmer who, along with a son and son-in-law, had to corner a skunk that had gotten into a chicken coop. During the confrontation, the skunk sprayed them in self-defense, hitting the farmer directly. The spray only slightly touched the farmer's son but it "penetrated" to his son-in-law—despite the fact that he had been shielded by the outside door of the chicken coop.

The reactions to the awfulness of skunk's smell varied. The farmer initially could not stand the odors on himself and he "gagged," yet he became amazed how quickly he became numb to the smell and could no longer sense it. His son, who had been sprayed slightly, could not stomach the smell in the least and began vomiting in reaction. His son-in-law, who had not been sprayed directly, became the most sickened by the odor.

Not until the farmer had killed the skunk and rid it from his life did he finally begin to notice the stench that permeated his clothes and person. When he became aware of this, it literally made him sick to his stomach and he began to vomit. His clothes were subsequently burned to rid him of the stench as much as possible, but even tomato soup and other efforts could not rid the smell from his person. It took a long time for the stench to wear off before he became free of it.

This is so like the experience of a transgressor. Choices that allow this "stench" into his life will quickly make him numb to the damage he is causing through sin—not only the damage to himself but to others around him. Initially, a transgressor cannot see the ugliness of his sins or how deeply he has transgressed; he only believes Satan's justifications and half-truths that his sins are trivial and of no consequence.

As a transgressor allows more and more light into his life and begins to see past choices in all their putridity, the depth and darkness of them will leave him disgusted, shaken, trembling and aghast at what he once felt were minor problems. This will be similar to Alma's experience when he came face to face with his sins. "I did remember all my sins and iniquities," he tells us,

> for which I was tormented with the pains of hell: yea, I saw that I had rebelled against my God, and that I had not kept his holy commandments.
>
> . . .In fine so great were my iniquities, that the very thought of coming into the presence of my God did rack my soul with inexpressible horror.
>
> Oh, thought I, that I could be banished and become extinct both soul and body, that I might not be brought to stand in the presence of my God, to be judged of my deeds. (Alma 36:13-15)

A transgressor *must* go through this type of self-awareness before attempts at healing can begin. He has to be able to see and acknowledge that he has been involved in damaging, destructive and dangerous sins that have devastated both his and his family's lives to great degree. Like the farmer who had to go to extensive efforts to rid his clothes and person from the skunk's scent, a transgressor must make serious and ongoing efforts to free himself from the sins that have seriously damaged his life and the lives of those surrounding him.

5

Cleansing: A Painful Process

Confession to the proper priesthood authority and to a wife is an essential step in the process of healing, but words cannot describe the devastation, heartache, pain, misery and trauma that a wife must go through when hearing or discovering the truth about a husband's sinful actions. Many times there is nothing that has prepared a soul to accept awful, agonizing realities that have been present in a relationship. Often a woman's heart will literally be shattered in facing these vicious, unexpected truths. As Jacob described it in the *Book of Mormon*, "Ye have broken the hearts of your tender wives. . .and the sobbings of their hearts ascend up to God against you." (Jacob 2:35) Also, he talks about these women having "daggers placed to pierce their souls and wound their delicate minds." (Jacob 2:9)

One woman described in private recordings her agony after her husband's confession: "I have lived a lifetime in the last few days. I've descended deeper than I ever have before in this life—than I ever thought I could. As I've heard the truth about the past, I've sometimes wished I could throw up and regurgitate from my body all the poison that seems to permeate my entire being from the intense filth I've had to listen to. Hearing the truth is literally sickening to my soul. I tremble at its ugliness. I've never felt a deeper sense of betrayal and pain. My implicit trust in my husband's faithfulness was violated in every regard. That brings with it deep pain that I know will only be healed through the Savior's atonement. I can only make it through this with Him."

The experience of hearing a husband's confession was also described by a woman this way: "I think I've tasted in a small degree what the Savior tasted during His suffering in the Garden. His was a pure soul that had to come face to face with evil and darkness that he had never experienced before in His life. I never imagined the darkness existed that I've had to face. It has shaken me to the core. It makes me realize in a tiny way what the Savior had to bear, and I've come to appreciate in a greater way what He did for us when he descended below all—when His pure soul took on all the ugliness that exists in the world. The small amount I tasted seemed more than I could bear, and it was only a tiny portion in relation to His suffering."

One woman said this about her husband's confession: "I went over and over again in my mind our past and our marriage. I kept thinking, 'I've been living a lie. This whole time, I've been living a lie.' It was so painful and unsettling to realize my husband's life had been filled with this kind of deception. I had loved and trusted him without restraint, yet he'd repeatedly betrayed me and our relationship. I felt like I couldn't trust my judgment in relation to him any more—or trust anything in our marriage. Why hadn't I seen what had occurred? How was it possible I'd missed it and hadn't sensed what had been going on? It took me a long time to feel like I had stepped back into reality instead of living in this numbed hazy shock that encompassed me after his confession. I still often struggle with the past and trying to work through what happened, attempting to view it all through a different lens than what I actually experienced at the time. It's very painful and unsettling to have to look at the past in that way."

Another reaction to a betrayal included these feelings: "For the longest time after finding out the truth [about my husband's actions], I could barely function. I would spend hours sobbing and felt terrible emotional pain. I couldn't eat and sleep. I felt so weary and tired as I suffered like this. I felt the pain and devastation as if I'd experienced a death. In some ways, I did experience a death. Nothing would ever be the same in my life or my relationship. Some days I could barely get through and take care of my children and the daily tasks I needed to accomplish. The only way I survived was by clinging to the strength that came from the Savior. If I didn't have a testimony of Him, I'm not sure I would have survived."

Another reaction to confession included intense anger and rage. "I felt so angry at my husband for the string of lies he'd told me and the years and years of deception he'd been involved in," one woman said. "I wanted to leave him and publicly humiliate him for what he'd done. It took me some time to overcome my anger over his betrayal and allow the Spirit to begin softening my heart so we could start to work things out. I still sometimes have a hard time overcoming the anger and resentment I feel for him because of his choices."

One woman spoke of the feelings she had when she discovered hundreds of pornographic sites on her husband's computer. "Suddenly I felt so dirty inside. It made me just sick thinking of all the times we had been intimate. I felt molested. I felt like I was filthy. I can't even begin to explain the depth of my feelings or exactly how bad I felt. The next few days I felt so numb. [My husband] was like a total stranger to me. I could not recognize him when I looked at him. I could not stand for him to touch me."

Truly, the time of confession and finding out vicious truths is a horrendous, devastating time for a wife. Yet only when she understands the depth of her husband's betrayal can the two of them move forward toward healing. The emotional trauma that ensues, however, will literally leave a woman enervated mentally, spiritually, physically and emotionally. There will be sleepless nights, desperate and agonizing deliberation, and physical trembling and trauma because of this terrible emotional suffering. There will be feelings of intense anger that come after knowledge of a betrayal. Uncertainty and confusion about the future and doubts about the possibility of healing become pervasive. Feelings of deep, inward, repugnance about the filthiness present in a relationship will bring physical, spiritual and emotional sickness.

Along with all of this suffering and emotion comes the inability to function effectively. It should be noted here that *no long-term decisions about the marriage and relationship should be made at this time of painful emotional reaction.* As one wise Bishop counseled a couple, "Do not make any decisions at all about your marriage relationship until you've given yourselves at least one month." This time period of waiting is essential. It will allow the wife to begin to get beyond the shock, devastation and anger surrounding a confession and begin to tune her heart and mind to the Savior's will for their family, whatever that entails, without making decisions that might be considered mistakes later on because of intense emotional confusion.

It is *imperative* to understand that *no one* can trust the emotion and feelings that come during the first several days after hearing a confession or finding out about a betrayal. This is a critical time in the relationship and Satan knows it. He has done this kind of damage before, and he knows how to further it. He knows the partner of a transgressor is reeling in emotional pain. He knows there is uncertainty, despair and fear as one looks to the future. He knows there is anger and resentment about the choices of another. He thus tries to become a powerful influence in the life of the one injured.

Satan tries to persuade an injured party to leave, to quit and to end the relationship where so much devastation and heartache has occurred. He tries to convince the partner that the marriage will inevitably fail and persuade that person to begin to work toward independence and living apart—that it is the only option now open. Or he may convince that person that a partner will continue to choose evil and thus ultimately choose to leave the marriage, anyway. He also tries to influence an injured party to tell the whole world about the sins of a partner so everyone can see how awful that transgressor is and how much trauma and damage has been inflicted by his choices. Satan will try over and over to sway this person into thinking that all these thoughts are coming from the Lord.

Satan does not want any type of healing to occur, so he will continue these types of cunning barrages. He will do everything in his power to destroy the marriage and the eternal family unit at this time. Not only does he continue to work tirelessly on the transgressor (who he already has a great hold on), but he will continue his unceasing assaults on the one who has been hurt and betrayed. As was noted earlier, a victim should never make essential critical decisions about a relationship during this period. Effective decisions can only be made when much-needed time has passed and the Lord and His Spirit have become part of the equation.

One woman, directly after her husband's confession, described her experiences this way: "When I found out about my husband's betrayal, it was as if Satan had been waiting for this precise moment to get to me. I remember my first clear thoughts that (thank goodness) I knew were from the adversary. They formed themselves perfectly in my mind. The adversary whispered to me, 'You don't have to take this. You can leave this situation. You deserve to leave after all your husband has done to you. He betrayed you and he lied to you. He deceived you. You don't have to take this. You can escape this mess. You deserve to escape this mess.' These thoughts were enticing to hear because they echoed my own feelings at the time. It seemed I suddenly had an 'out' to the incredible pain and heartache I was experiencing. I wanted to pack up and leave my husband and take my children away from his awful influence. I even remember I wanted to tell the whole world—especially my family—what a bad person my husband was. I was so angry at him.

"I am so grateful that my Bishop cautioned me to wait until making any sort of decision about the future. He also cautioned me strongly about sharing information that later could be damaging to my husband if he did repent. This gave me the time and space I needed to step back and let the Savior's Spirit come into my life and direct me, as I needed Him to do.

"I had some powerful spiritual experiences afterward which taught me amazing eternal principles. I felt so grateful I hadn't left my husband because of Satan's promptings. I came to learn that I had been given a foreordained mission to help him here on earth to overcome his problems and addictions. If I had left him initially I would not have fulfilled one of the callings the Lord had given me to accomplish in this life. As I turned to the Lord in my thoughts instead of listening to the adversary's escape routes, the Savior's impressions and insights continued.

"I began to slowly heal from my deep wounds. Soon I could reach out and help my husband—even amidst my pain—in beginning to heal our damaged relationship. We are not completely healed and we have a long road ahead of us, but we have made great strides and are working hard to overcome the problems between us."

The Prophet Joseph Smith gave some wise, eternal counsel regarding discovering the sins of a transgressor. He said,

> At this time, the truth on the guilty should not be told openly, strange as this may seem, yet this is a policy. We must use precaution in bringing sinners to justice, lest in exposing these heinous sins we draw the indignation of [the] world upon us. . . .To the iniquitous show yourselves merciful.
> . . .I do not want to cloak iniquity—all things contrary to the will of God, should be cast

from us, but don't do more hurt than good with your tongues—be pure in heart. (*Teachings*, p. 239)

In summary, then, confession in a relationship is essential in beginning the process of healing, but it will not be easy getting through this emotionally devastating time. The partner must remember to let time pass before any crucial decisions are made about the marriage. Reactions must be tempered carefully with time and through the Spirit. During this period, too, the one injured must carefully guard against the whisperings and promptings of the adversary, whose only intent is to destroy a family—not to heal one. His solutions and escapes will never bring the wholeness sought for but will only bring about further heartache and increased devastation.

The First Inklings of Peace

Another insight to note about confession is that there will not be any feelings of peace at all about a relationship *until the confession is sufficient for that time*. Remember, as said in an earlier chapter, that truth will never come out all at once and there will be ongoing "confession" sessions as more sins are remembered. But when a husband is truly trying to confess and gets to the point of needed confession during those initial stages of "coming clean," there is a tangible feeling of peace that comes with it. It will give a partner the first feeling of hope and confidence that a healing might be able to occur in a marriage.

When a husband is lying, trying to hide or continuing deception or "glossing" of sins, *this peace will not come*. There is still troubled anxiety, distrust and feelings of unsettled distress. One woman shares her experience this way: "I kept confronting my husband and asking him to tell me the truth [about his pornography addiction], but he kept lying to me. I knew innately he was lying. Finally, I got packed up and was ready to leave. I had no desire to stay with someone as repulsive and un-humble as he was. He didn't seem to care at all about the hurt I was experiencing or that he had crushed me by what he'd done.

"We had the worst fight that night that we've ever had. I told him I didn't need him—that he was 'filthy' and that I was 'better off alone.' When he finally could see I was serious and on the verge of leaving, he finally broke down and began sobbing. He apologized. He told me he would do whatever it took to make our marriage right again.

"I think my being ready to leave is what forced his confession. I'm not sure he would have told me had I not been willing to go. He finally told me the whole truth about what he'd been involved in. I had been sustained by adrenaline up until then, but when the whole truth finally came out, I collapsed in his arms."

For another woman, it got to the point when she could sense through the Spirit when her husband was lying to her or when he was attempting to tell the truth. Instead of trusting what she heard from his mouth or his assertions alone, she always weighed his words on an inward scale, trying to discern from the Spirit what was truth and what was not. She came to sense immediately when he was lying and then could confront him at those times. The Lord promises:

> For behold, my brethren, it is given unto you to judge, that ye may know good from evil; and the way to judge is as plain, that ye may know with a perfect knowledge, as the daylight is from the dark night.
>
> For behold, the Spirit of Christ is given to every man, that he may know good from evil; wherefore, I show unto you the way to judge; for every thing which inviteth to do good, and to persuade to believe in Christ, is sent forth by the power and gift of Christ; wherefore ye may know with a perfect knowledge it is of God.
>
> But whatsoever thing persuadeth men to do evil, and believe not in Christ, and deny him, and serve not God, then ye may know with a perfect

knowledge it is of the devil; for after this manner
doth the devil work, for he persuadeth no man to
do good, no not one; neither do his angels; neither
do they who subject themselves unto him. (Moroni
7:15-17)

Truly, those working with transgressors will have the
first inklings of peace when they know sufficient truth for that
moment. One woman recalls the time when she heard her
husband's confessions during a trying, three-day period when
she first learned the truth about his past. She says, "During this
time, I had not had one feeling of peace but only felt further and
more deeply troubled by what I kept learning about his past."
Finally, one morning—after she'd heard a few more necessary
details of her husband's past indiscretions, she suddenly felt
an incredible feeling of peace wash over her. "Into my mind,
as this peace came, I saw a powerful visible image. It was
almost as if I could see the inside of my husband's soul and the
Savior's light beginning to penetrate it. I could see this powerful
light literally sifting through my husband's insides, starting at
his heart and then moving onward to permeate the pockets
of darkness that had been hidden inside. The image was so
powerful and compelling that it literally left me breathless. As
I basked in this, I felt the certain knowledge that my husband
was being cleansed through the power of the atonement and
that he would ultimately be cleansed. This was the first glimmer
of hope I had that our relationship could heal. I was so grateful
for the image and insight given to me from the Savior at that
time. It gave me something to cling to through the following
days of horrendous trials and problems so I could hold on to
the certainty that one day my husband would be clean."
     It needs to be noted that often feelings of peace or hope
will come in abundance at the beginning of the confession
period, *but this does not indicate that the healing is complete.* It
indicates that healing has begun. These feelings and impressions
are anchors of hope and the light of promised eternal blessings

that will occur in the future. Remember: These are glimpses of the future, not indications of present healing. Healing has only begun; it has not been completed. A long, painful road lies ahead and it will not be trodden quickly or easily.

There are patterns of thought, behaviors and actions that need to be overcome; there are addictive habits that a husband still grapples with—and will certainly fall victim to— before he overcomes his addiction; and there are many, many problems and strains on a relationship that don't suddenly disappear. These issues have to be dissolved one by one, idea by idea and step by step. But with confession and these feelings of peace, rest assured that the right steps have been taken and the necessary beginnings of the path to wholeness have been found.

One woman described it this way: "After finding out about my husband's sins, we were given a two-week period of an incredibly close relationship. It was wonderful and healing—beyond anything we'd had before. After this two weeks ended, we plummeted. We went to the depths. It was as if the Lord had given us a wonderful cake to eat and now this cake was gone. What I'm learning now is that slowly, idea by idea and step by step, the Lord is giving us the ingredients to make that cake again. We now know what it tastes like and what it will be like, and we're slowly being given the tools to build our relationship once more." Indeed, hope and light after a confession are temporary, but they are true indications of what can and will be if both partners continue faithful and true in turning to the Savior for healing.

A Confession Caution

As noted above, confession is the first step toward healing, but it is only the first step in this long road of recovery and healing. Many other painful and difficult steps will occur afterward, not only for the transgressor but the innocent people around him who will have to suffer through the cleansing process. They, too, have been subjected to evil and darkness because of a transgressor's choices and must overcome it in their personal lives.

A strong caution needs to be made during the initial stages of confession and forsaking of sin. Even with honest, truthful and open confessions by a transgressor, *there will always be relapses*—relapses in actions, thoughts and behaviors that led a transgressor to the point where he is at. Just as we grow line upon line, so do we heal line upon line. Healing will *never* be immediate and complete. There will still be problems, contention, anger and blame; there will still be damaging thoughts, behaviors and actions. Unless these relapses are seen as speed bumps along the path—not as detours that cannot be overcome—there will no lasting healing.

Steven A. Cramer in *Putting on the Armor of God* says it in the following way. Although he is speaking directly to those involved in masturbation, this may be used as a "warning" for all transgressors:

> . . .No matter how great the determination is to break free, . . .there are likely to be occasional relapses. You should not panic when this happens because it is a normal part of growth and change. The demons hope that when you slip you will sink into despair, condemn yourself and doubt the principles of spiritual warfare. You must not let them defeat you with feelings of self-condemnation and guilt. An occasional mistake while you are healing is not the same as deliberately choosing the evil way. If you are determined to defeat Satan and persist in your efforts, your relapses will grow further and further apart until total victory is achieved. (pp. 279-280)

This must be remembered in dealing effectively with the continuing efforts of a transgressor in trying to overcome sin. It should be noted, however, that if a transgressor adopts a non-caring attitude about his problems and still continues to point the blame for continuing contention or other behaviors toward a spouse, *healing has stopped*. As the Lord has said, "He that hath the spirit of contention is not of me, but is of the devil, who is the father of contention, and he stirreth up the hearts of men to contend with anger, one with another." (3 Nephi 11: 29) Healing will not continue until contention is overcome and a repentant, humble attitude is adopted by the transgressor.

Wounds of the Innocent

As mentioned earlier, transgressors' actions never hurt only themselves, but they have hurt and will continue to hurt those innocent parties in the home—wives, children or others who are subjected to the evil influences of transgressors' choices without having realized it. An example of how the evil spirits alone can influence and damage the atmosphere of the home and thus harm innocent parties is so beautifully illustrated in the book *One Tattered Angel* by Blaine M. Yorgason.

Blaine Yorgason, his wife and his family had the opportunity to adopt a beautiful little girl, Charity, who had been born with severe handicaps—no brain and only a brain stem which basically ran the autonomic nervous system in her body. Though the family had been told by the doctors that Charity "wouldn't be able to see, hear, feel, taste, or smell," that "she would know nothing of what was going on around her; would never have any control over any part of her body; would never experience or be able to express joy, happiness, and love; and would simply live her life in a vegetative state," (p. 43) this simply was not the case. Charity indeed felt emotions and pain; she visibly reacted to sounds and people; even once she had twenty minutes of giggling and smiling. The family deeply loved and enjoyed her and interacted with her often.

They often dealt with Charity's pains and sicknesses because of her physical problems, but one sickness in particular became troubling to the father. He described this time as follows:

During one of her "good times," Charity suddenly grew very ill. We couldn't tell what was wrong, the doctors couldn't tell, and even Tylenol didn't bring her any peace. She was absolutely miserable.

Of course, we prayed constantly for help in knowing what to do, but for a week we remained at a loss. Then one Saturday morning while I was pleading for her relief, it suddenly dawned on me that the problem might not be Charity's. Quickly I gathered the family into an emergency session.

"All right, listen up. You all know that Charity is doing badly. Since we can't seem to find a problem with her, I'm thinking that maybe the problem is with one of us."

"What are you talking about, Dad?"

"I'm talking about the fact that she is perfectly pure, without sin. Do you all agree with me?"

Everyone nodded.

"Okay, do you all agree that she will never, no matter how long she lives, have the capacity or desire to commit sin?"

"We all know that, Dad." Dan's mind was racing ahead like always. "What's the point?"

". . .The point is that Charity is truly a heavenly person, the only one I've ever known. In terms of purity, at least, she is just like God, whom the Bible says is perfect. And since God doesn't like sin, what do you suppose might happen if Charity is forced to be around it?"

"She wouldn't like it," Michelle declared.

"How would she let us know she didn't like it? How would she react? Think about this, kids. Suppose one or more of us is doing something wrong. I don't mean the normal little stuff. I mean something pretty major that our conscience is already telling us we shouldn't be doing. With Charity being unable to get away from us because of her circumstances, and being unable to tolerate our sins because of her perfect purity, might her reaction be to get sick?"

Everybody looked at me in amazement, Kathy [his wife] included.

"Remember," I went on, "I'm not suggesting that we need to be perfect. But I believe we each need to go off alone for a few minutes and search our souls. If I'm right, one of us is having a major problem with sin that we're hiding—only apparently we can't hide it from Charity. If it happens to be you, come tell me quickly, and let's get this taken care of before she suffers any further."

A few moments later one of the kids came quietly into my office, acknowledged an inappropriate book hidden in the home, and asked what should be done. My instructions—and I was playing this completely by ear—were to take the book to where it came from, apologize to Charity, and then go off alone and apologize to God and seek His forgiveness.

My counsel was strictly followed, and thirty minutes after that Charity was smiling and happy again, with no signs of her former illness about her.

Time and again we observed this phenomenon. Charity reacted almost instantly to wickedness around her—she was not physically able to tolerate it. (pp. 86-88)

This is a powerful illustration of the effect evil choices can have in the atmosphere of a home. Evil spirits and influences are literally allowed into a home when certain sins occur. This is a true, valid concept. The sins of one can affect the whole family within the bounds of that eternal family relationship, whether or not they are physically present in the place where the transgression is occurring.

In one home, for example, before the truth about her husband's continuing participation in pornography came out, one woman suddenly began struggling with intense feelings of darkness and discouragement, never feeling as if she was able to fight these feelings and find the source. She often felt depressed, discouraged and downhearted without knowing why. As she was going through her own trying set of emotions, her older daughter often had blatant physical displays of a slight medical problem, feeling the need to get desired attention. A younger daughter complained of incessant nightmares and often couldn't sleep without lights on or without being near someone else. The son in the family had been going to school pretending he had a broken arm; he had wrapped it in a removable cast and professed to be unable to do his schoolwork. His "injury" was only brought to his mother's attention when someone asked his mother when he was going to "heal."

This mother looked back in amazement at what had happened during this time as she realized all these behaviors and problems had occurred when her husband had fallen back into his pornography addiction. Only when he confessed once again and tried to overcome his addiction did she feel these evil influences in the home begin to lessen. The accompanying difficult issues they had experienced lessened, as well, and her children seemed more at peace, happier and more secure. She tied these feelings directly to the attempts to overcome the pornography problems her husband had fallen victim to once more.

Many women harbor deep, unseen wounds from the darkness that has plagued homes where there have been pornography addictions. Some of these wounds may resurface in such things as a low self-concept, lack of self-confidence or poor self-esteem. Many become obsessed with their bodies, never feeling like their physical appearance will be adequate or sufficient unless they work relentlessly on it. So often women who have lived with pornography addicts in their homes will have breast augmentation or other surgeries to enhance physical appearance. Even afterward, many will continually struggle with feelings of inadequacy. Sometimes, too, women will gain weight in reaction to the problems in the home, turning to food for comfort and solace.

One woman spoke of these types of wounds after finding out about her husband's pornography problem: "I had always felt physically attractive in my life," she said. "Appearance had never been a huge issue to me. I felt like Heavenly Father had blessed me with a good and shapely body and although a small amount of my self-esteem was tied up with this, I never obsessed about it.

"After I found out about my husband, however, [his problem with pornography], everything totally changed. I felt like I could never 'live up' again. I felt completely worthless. At first, Satan worked hard on me. He convinced me I should never have kids or it would ruin my figure. I felt I needed to work out every day and go tanning—do everything I could to have a beautiful body. I felt like I needed to have surgery to enhance my physical appearance.

"I suddenly came to the realization that if I focused on this 'physical' part of me like I was, I would lose the 'spiritual' part of me—even my desire to have kids. I decided then that I was going to refuse to try to live up to a 'robot.' I had to keep constantly turning to spiritual things so I could overcome.

"To this day, I still feel like I can never live up. If I see a scantily clad or voluptuous woman, it's like a trigger point that causes me to come crashing down. I still hate going to pools and seeing women there. It makes me feel like my physical appearance will always be less than wonderful."

Women are not the only ones who suffer internal injuries like this. Children truly feel and sense darkness brought in by transgression, whether or not they can articulate it. There are many outside indications they sense it. Many become whiney, seek attention in detrimental ways, begin to wet the bed, begin troubled behavioral patterns, become aggressive, etc. They may often complain of nightmares, have unexplained fears, or become "clingy." Though this occurs partly because of the contention and stress that may be occurring in a marriage, this is not the only influence harming them. Darkness from others' choices can and will permeate a home and injure all who are within it or bound by eternal family ties.

One woman came to realize that one of her sons had become tormented by darkness and evil brought in by her husband's sins when her son began the practice of masturbation and had unrelenting unclean thoughts put incessantly into his mind. Although masturbation is often common in teens and cannot always be directly related to pornography addictions, this woman came to feel her son struggled because of the spirits her husband brought into the home.

In studying transgressors and their families, this phenomenon has occurred again and again. Innocent parties have become subject to the darkness and damage brought in by the unrighteous choices of others. Until they know the reason this darkness and damage has occurred, they won't truly heal or become effective in casting this darkness out. Once awareness has occurred, however, needed keys for ridding these influences from lives can be adopted. These keys are found in such things as priesthood blessings, the playing of hymns, prayers for protection, temple attendance, scripture reading, attending church meetings and other righteous efforts. Consistent spiritual efforts are truly the most effective weapons in safeguarding a home and family from evil and darkness.

Sin Can Expose A Transgressor and Those Around Him to Physical Danger and Harm

The idea that sin can expose a transgressor and those innocent parties around him to actual physical danger and harm can be illustrated from examples found in the *Book of Mormon*. One example occurs during the time when Lehi, Nephi, Laman and Lemuel and their families were crossing the ocean to the promised land. At one point during the journey, Nephi's brothers "and the sons of Ishmael began to make themselves merry, insomuch that they began to dance, and to sing, and to speak with much rudeness, yea, even that they did forget by what power they had been brought thither; yea, they were lifted up unto exceeding rudeness." (1 Nephi 18:9) Nephi warned them about their iniquities, but they did not stop. This opened them up—even the innocent parties around them—to actual physical harm. Nephi tells us that

> there arose a great and terrible tempest, and we were driven back upon the waters for the space of three days; and they began to be frightened exceedingly lest they should be drowned in the sea.
>
> . . .And on the fourth day, which we had been driven back, the tempest began to be exceedingly sore.
>
> And it came to pass that we were about to be swallowed up in the depths of the sea. . . .My brethren began to see that the judgments of God were upon them, and that they must perish save that they should repent of their iniquities. (1 Nephi 18:13-15)

Nephi and all the other innocent parties on that ship were subjected to physical harm because of the unrighteous actions of others. Others' wickedness directly affected the physical safety of those in the family. This can happen in the lives and circumstances of any transgressor.

Another example of this physical affliction occurs when Lehi and his family traveled in the wilderness. Alma says of this time that "they. . .did not travel a direct course, and were *afflicted with hunger and thirst*, because of their transgressions." (Alma 37:42, italics added) These were, once again, physical afflictions brought about by spiritual choices, affecting all parties—even innocent ones not responsible for wickedness.

In Jacob 3:10 it says to transgressors, "Ye shall remember your children, how that ye have grieved their hearts because of the example ye have set before them; and also, remember that ye may, because of your filthiness, bring your children unto destruction, and their sins be heaped upon your heads at the last day." Though this is assuredly speaking of the spiritual ramifications and consequences of sin, we strongly believe that physical harm and destruction can be inferred from this, as well. *Transgressors' sins can bring physical harm and damage to the innocent parties surrounding them.*

As an example, this kind of physical harm and destruction occurred when a man had an affair after a life-long addiction to pornography. During the time of his undiscovered sins, his sons were in a terrible car accident and almost lost their lives. The mother in the family came to believe that they were subjected to this physical harm because of her husband's choices.

One woman looked back at the times her husband admitted he had participated in sins during their marriage, and she realized in amazement how many of those times were directly related to physical, financial or other difficulties that had arisen within her home and family. One time, a frightening prank phone call occurred in which her safety and the safety of her children had been threatened; other times, there were multitudes of physical problems with cars and home repairs which seemed directly related to his indiscretions. There were also times of intense struggle financially that she could see were directly correlated to times when he had slipped and fallen into transgression.

From this it cannot be inferred that all physical problems and struggles are caused by sin. We, as temporal beings, are subject to these naturally because of our physical state. However, it is interesting to take note of how many problems and physical dangers occur for innocent parties when there is transgression present in a home. As Lehi said to his sons, "Nothing, save it shall be iniquity among [you], shall harm or disturb [your] prosperity on the face of this land forever." (2nd Nephi 1:31) Iniquity, however, can harm and disturb prosperity "among you," including the prosperity of innocent parties.

When Wounds Become too Great to Bear

Sometimes innocent parties who have been wounded by the transgressions of others cannot get beyond the hurt, devastation, resentment, anger, injuries and pain they've experienced to move toward healing. Perhaps they do well for a time but then memories will haunt them; the future seems bleak and dark; the inability to "forgive and forget" seems impossible; emotions and the inability to function resurface; and they cannot move forward in their relationship toward healing.

Just as transgressors have times when they are literally powerless over controlling emotions, thoughts and behaviors, so do victims have times when they cannot control their feelings, attitudes, and emotions. Evil spirits will work overtime during these periods, especially when they see victims vulnerable and hurting. The adversary tries to convince victims that moving forward is fruitless and impossible—that nothing will ever improve and that their efforts will not make a difference. This leaves them in a sea of darkness, discouragement and despair, making it seem as if they'll never be able to overcome trials in their lives.

These times need to be turned into times of fasting, deep introspection and reaching to the Lord in fervent, pleading prayer to get beyond the despondency they will find themselves in. Just as transgressors must have the strength of the Lord to overcome their difficulties, so will these injured parties need the strength of the Lord to have Him heal wounds they cannot overcome on their own. They cannot do it alone or move forward without His sustaining hand. He cautions, "Verily, verily, I say unto you, *ye must watch and pray always*, lest ye be tempted by the devil, and ye be led away captive by him." (3rd Nephi 18:15)

Remember, the Lord invites His children to lay their burdens at His feet. He tells us, "Come unto me all ye that labour and are heavy laden, and I will give you rest.

"Take my yoke upon you, and learn of me; for I am meek

and lowly in heart: and ye shall find rest unto your souls.

"For my yoke is easy, and my burden is light." (Matthew 11:28-30) Psalms 55:22 echoes this invitation: "Cast thy burden upon the Lord, and he shall sustain thee: he shall never suffer the righteous to be moved."

Through intense reaching and persistent supplication to the Lord, injured parties can trust that the pain and uncertainty they feel inside can subside, knowing the Lord will not leave them alone or comfortless. (John 14:18) They can know He will help them step by step—sometimes inch by inch—in moving forward. They can go on with "peace. . .unto [their] soul(s)," knowing that their "adversity and affliction shall be but a small moment;

"And then, if [they] endure it well, God shall exalt [them] on high; [they] shalt triumph over all their foes." (D&C 121:7-8) They can rest on the assurance that the Lord, as with the people of Alma, will walk with them during their afflictions. He promises:

> . . .Lift up your heads and be of good comfort, for I know of the covenant which ye have made unto me; and I will covenant with my people and deliver them out of bondage.
>
> And I will also ease the burdens which are put upon your shoulders, that even you cannot feel them upon your backs, even while you are in bondage; and this will I do that ye may stand as witnesses for me hereafter, and that ye may know of a surety that I, the Lord God, do visit my people in their afflictions.
>
> And now it came to pass that the burdens which were laid upon Alma and his brethren were made light; yea, the Lord did strengthen them that they could bear up their burdens with ease, and they did submit cheerfully and with patience to all the will of the Lord. (Mosiah 24:13-15)

And now, my brethren, I desire that ye shall plant this word in your hearts, and as it beginneth to swell even so nourish it by your faith. And behold, it will become a tree, springing up in you unto everlasting life. And then may God grant unto you that your burdens may be light, through the joy of his Son. (Alma 33:23)

6

Insights Into a Transgressor

With the acknowledgement and confession of a problem with pornography, a transgressor has indeed begun the road to healing—but often this step is seen as complete repentance and recovery by the transgressor. He many times does not realize he has a multitude of other steps and efforts that need to be taken to move toward full healing and repentance. One woman described it this way: "When we first married, it was as if I gave a gift to my husband of innate trust. This gift could be compared to a thick, solid, high brick wall that became his freely and unconditionally when we said our vows across the altar. When he sinned, however, it was as if he took a monster crane and wrecking ball and literally smashed the brick wall with it. Now, in order to get back that trust, this wall has to be built brick by brick again. Any repeated indiscretions knock that wall completely down, and it has to be started from the bottom once more."

This rebuilding "brick by brick" is a wonderful analogy of the time, effort and work it will take to overcome all the damage and injury that has been done by a transgressor. Repentance cannot be seen as immediate or complete only when acknowledgement and confession of the problem has occurred, even if church action has been taken against a transgressor. Herein lies a trap for most men who have sinned. Many transgressors think they are done, finished and have overcome their problems by walking these miniscule first steps.

They think their wives should be done and finished, as well. They may often claim, when there are continuing problems and questions in their relationship regarding integrity, actions, behaviors, decisions and attitudes, "Wait a minute. I've done my part. I've confessed and come clean. I've paid my price with the Lord and the Church. You're not forgiving me. You don't trust me. You have the problem now. I've done what I needed to do and you're the one that keeps holding on to this and holding it over my head. It's not fair of you to act like that or feel as if I'm off base. I'm not. You're the one that's off base because of your contention and anger toward me; you keep bringing up problems of the past. I've paid my price and I'm done. You need to forgive me and let it go. That's the only problem now—your lack of forgiveness and your distrust of me and where I'm at."

Steven A. Cramer in his book *The Worth of A Soul*, stated that:

> Most people take their sins too lightly. In these days of "instant" everything we too often expect to dismiss our sins with a quick sigh of remorse as we rush on to the next experience. President Kimball has warned that many people "have no conception of satisfying the Lord, of paying the total penalties and obtaining a release and adjustment which could be considered final and which might be accepted of the Lord." (*Miracle of Forgiveness*, p. 156)
>
> "Your Heavenly Father has promised forgiveness upon total repentance and meeting all the requirements, but that forgiveness is not granted

merely for the asking. There must be works—many
works—and an all-out, total surrender, with a great
humility and a 'broken heart and a contrite spirit.' "
(*Ibid. p. 324*) (p. 121)

Problems and contention in a marriage will escalate
and become insurmountable unless a transgressor truly adopts
an attitude of complete humility and a willingness to work
hard and unceasingly to overcome past sins and indiscretions.
No further steps will be made in the healing process if the
transgressor cannot accept the fact that for a long period
of his life he has not had the influence of the Spirit and has
adopted attitudes, ideas and behaviors that are not consistent
with the gospel of Jesus Christ. Thinking has been tainted and
ideas skewed by the darkness of the adversary. "Pride" and
"selfishness" have become governing traits, as well. (D&C 56:
8) A transgressor must understand the intense efforts that will
be needed to overcome these ideas and behaviors instead of
believing confession has made the healing process complete.

Blame, manipulation, anger and control have become
integral parts of a personality and cannot be immediately
and instantaneously overcome, either. Overcoming is a long,
arduous, painful and time-consuming process, one that will
require much patience on the part of the wife and others in the
home. Unless the transgressor sees this process for the hardship
that it is and accepts his responsibility for his part in creating
the difficulties that have arisen, relationships and marriages will
never heal. Phil S. in *The Perfect Brightness of Hope*, an impacting
book describing his struggles as an LDS person overcoming his
powerful addiction to alcohol and other sins, said it this way:

The more we addicts deny our own
accountability, the more we lock ourselves in guilt
and addiction. This fact is critical to both addict
and co-dependent: Regardless of our circumstances,
if we want to stop hurting and begin recovering,

*we must come to an absolute acceptance that no one
is responsible for the misery and unmanageability of
our lives except ourselves.* If we continue to insist
on focusing outward, blaming others and external
circumstances, we will remain powerless in the one
thing we *can* change—ourselves! (p. 179)

Counseling with the proper priesthood authorities is
essential during this time, and often the counsel and guidance
of trained professionals is needed. Counselors and priesthood
holders can give basic guidelines to help a transgressor become
more aware of how his thoughts, actions, attitudes and behaviors
are skewed and distorted. They can affirm that overcoming is
a difficult, ongoing process, and that there will be needed life-
long changes and efforts to be made from this point onward.
They can also help a transgressor discover that it is not only
a process of overcoming sin, but a process of rebuilding and
adopting righteous attitudes and practices that is necessary.
They can help a transgressor become more resistant to future
transgression by pointing out weaknesses and vulnerabilities
that have led a transgressor to sin in the past.

It should be reasserted at this juncture that the
humility of a transgressor is truly the first step toward healing
a marriage, no matter how willing and determined a partner is
to move forward. *No progress will be made in a relationship if an
attitude of humility is not adopted by a transgressor.* This is not to
say that a wife must feel as if she cannot move forward on her
own toward healing, but it is to say that the *relationship* will not
move forward toward healing unless this occurs.

If a transgressor is not willing or cannot humble himself
on his own, often the Lord will take steps during this time to
humble a transgressor through ongoing difficulties, hardships
and trials. The Lord knows it is only through humility that
He can work with one's heart to change him. As He said in
the scriptures, "I will lift him up inasmuch as he will humble
himself before me." (D&C 106:7) If needs be, the Lord will

use financial difficulties, strains in work or other relationships, physical hardships or other trials to bring needed humility into a transgressor's life. It is far better to adopt this needed attribute on one's own instead of being "compelled to be humble," (Alma 32:15) as others have had to be. The Lord loves a transgressor so deeply that He will do everything He can to bring this type of humility into a transgressor's life so that healing can begin.

Understanding Thought Patterns and Vulnerabilities

Another important step a transgressor must take in overcoming his problems is to begin to understand, discern and become aware of the thought patterns, attitudes, weaknesses and ideas that have made him vulnerable to the sins which have held him captive. He must also become aware of places, times, circumstances and factors that have contributed to his transgressions. It is imperative to come to this kind of self-awareness in order to stop the damage that has occurred—and will keep occurring—unless this type of understanding comes about. As the scriptures say,

> There is nothing from without a man, that entering into him can defile him: but the things which come out of him, those are they that defile the man.
> . . .For from within, out of the heart of men, proceed evil thoughts, adulteries, fornications, murders, . . .covetousness, wickedness, deceit, lasciviousness, an evil eye, blasphemy, pride foolishness:
> All these evil things come from within, and defile the man. (Mark 7:15, 21-23)

Understanding these types of thought patterns and vulnerabilities is the first crucial step toward arresting sinful behavior. As one Bishop so aptly claimed, "self-hatred" is often the precursor to transgression. Feelings of discouragement and depression are the two most common weaknesses that go hand and hand with this self-hatred and often contribute to a transgressor's need for a temporary "fix" of short-lived gratification.

Other factors that might lead to transgression include pride, lack of humility and arrogance. These attitudes drive away the influence of the Spirit and open up a life to Satan's temptations and influence. Attempting to compensate for deficiencies in the past or seeking fulfillment because of wounds received during childhood can be other factors contributing to a vulnerability to transgression, as well.

"Self-hatred," once again, can often be seen in the discouragement, depression, guilt, self-disgust, self-loathing, lack of confidence and fear that either precedes or follows transgression. It was stated this way in the October 2002 *New Era:* "Guilt, fear and depression are common emotions for those involved with pornography—guilt, because they know what they are doing is wrong; fear, because they are terrified their secret will be found out; and depression, because they no longer feel the Spirit. Relationships with family, friends, Church leaders, and the Lord are damaged." (p. 34) These thoughts and attitudes are often precursors to sin or are perpetuated by continuing sin.

Unchecked pride, lack of humility and arrogance are other precursors to sin. These attitudes can be seen in such things as the love of "riches and the vain things of the world" (Helaman 7:21); the inability to be able to see one's own weaknesses and shortfalls; an unwillingness to hear or listen to the righteous counsel of God and His servants; a hard and unyielding heart; unabated contention, harshness and anger toward others in relationships; bitterness toward others who may show weaknesses or flaws, etc. As it says so aptly in the scriptures, "Beware of pride, lest thou shouldst enter into temptation." (D&C 23:1)

Another factor that can make someone vulnerable to transgression occurs when that person is attempting to compensate for deficiencies in the past—such as a lack of unconditional love, nurturing, kindness or affection—in damaging, unhealthy ways. Some seeking fulfillment or comfort from wounds or injuries received from childhood may begin to look for it through destructive practices. All these lacks or emotional deficits can make someone vulnerable to Satan's whisperings and deceits when they attempt to fulfill these unmet needs.

Each transgressor must come to see the individual areas in which he is weak and susceptible before he can begin to heal. Often Bishops or professional counselors can help with this kind of self-awareness in a transgressor, pointing out erroneous patterns and ideas they might have incorporated into their lives. They may help transgressors begin to see the times and circumstances in their lives that Satan sees as conducive to temptation and sin. Awareness of these factors becomes a huge step toward recovery and will bring about great strides in the healing process.

As one man started going through his repentance process, he began to become more aware of his thought patterns and attitudes—those ideas and feelings that would make him susceptible to the mistakes he had often made in the past. He began to see how his thoughts would "drift" and become different right before he would go out of town for business—the environment in which all of his transgressions had occurred previously. The adversary would plant in his mind continuing ideas that would make him discouraged, depressed, despondent and feeling sorry for himself. He began to be surprised at the intensity, clarity and specific pattern of these thoughts. He slowly began to see and discern how the feelings these thoughts created had made him vulnerable to seeking the gratification and escape he had sought through sin. Only by stopping the thoughts in the very initial stages was he able to begin to overcome the grip Satan had won on his heart. So it must be with each transgressor. Each must begin to understand the thought patterns, behaviors and attitudes that begin the fall downward before he can effectively eradicate them.

Acknowledging the Existence of a Double Life

A transgressor must also come to discern and acknowledge the existence of the double life he has been leading in order to make any headway in healing. A double life could be seen as "double lies" in two major aspects of his life. On one hand, he has been—or pretended to be—a hard-working, likable and responsible person, acting normal and ordinary in almost all aspects of "outward" living. All this time, however, he has been living a lie. He has another secret, hidden, deplorable life he hides that is full of sin, hypocrisy and deceit.

A transgressor must see and openly acknowledge how damaging this double life has been to himself and others. For one thing, he has lost the influence and rights of the priesthood in his life. "The rights of the priesthood are inseparably connected with the powers of heaven," the Lord has told us.

> . . .*When we undertake to cover our sins,* or to gratify our pride, our vain ambition, or to exercise control or dominion or compulsion upon the souls of the children of men, in any degree of unrighteousness, behold, the heavens withdraw themselves; the Spirit of the Lord is grieved; and when it is withdrawn, *Amen to the priesthood or authority of that man.* (D&C 121:37, italics added)

Covenants have been broken and severed by these hidden sins, as well. "As the covenant which they made unto me has been broken, *even so it has become void and of none effect,*" it says in D&C 54:4 (italics added). A transgressor, in essence, is no longer sealed to his wife and family in a covenant relationship because of his sins. This needs to be acknowledged.

A transgressor needs to understand, too, that he is incapable of pure love and healthy relationships until he has learned to "bridle all [his] passions." It is only when this is done that he "may be filled with love" (Alma 38:12) and build meaningful family bonds.

A transgressor must also understand the depth of his sins. He has so often convinced himself that the double life he has been leading is so miniscule that he does not realize the tremendous damage and disastrous consequences of his sinful acts. Many times, like one transgressor, transgressors feel like they might have just been "looking over the fence" without truly partaking or deeply sinning. "Ye are not justified, because these things are among you," the Lord warns. (D&C 63:19) "Let such beware and repent speedily, lest judgment shall come upon them as a snare, and their folly shall be made manifest, and their works shall follow them in the eyes of the people." (D&C 63:16)

Helping a Wife and Children Begin to Heal

Another step in the repentance and healing process of a transgressor is the necessity of seeing clearly the damage one has caused to a wife and children through unrighteous choices. A transgressor must realize that he has lost the Spirit in almost all of his interactions. He has wounded and hurt those around him—knowingly or unknowingly. His relationships must be built anew—on a different foundation of love, patience, caring and understanding, not the negativity, criticism, impatience, anger, control, blame and manipulation these relationships have been built on before.

This "building" requires a willingness and resolution of a transgressor to begin to help in the healing process of innocent victims surrounding him. A transgressor must learn to avoid the contention, blame or anger that have been his first and ready reactions to problems. He must learn to listen— repeatedly, if necessary—to his wife's concerns and wounds. He must learn to do this with patience and without becoming resentful of her need to talk or openly express her distrust, her feelings of anger and her sense of betrayal. He must work with her and be patient with her inability to forgive immediately his transgressions. He must understand her overreactions to problems when she begins to see echoes of earlier behaviors that have led him to sin.

He also must understand, if there are recurrences of sinful behavior, that a wife won't be perfect in her responses and will often resort to intense anger, resentment and judgment. Though these reactions may be considered "wrong," as well, a transgressor must be as patient and forgiving of these as he is in the expectations of forgiveness for himself and his own mistakes. As one Bishop counseled a transgressor, "If it takes throughout eternity for your wife to be healed, it is now your job to do it because of your choices."

A transgressor must learn to put aside his own judgment in most situations to hear the insights, rationale and perceptions of his wife, who will often have greater access to spiritual light and knowledge at this time in their healing. If a transgressor can make what he initially sees as these "emotional sacrifices" in establishing these things in a relationship, the beginnings of trust, love and true sharing can finally begin. This won't happen until the transgressor is humble in accepting his weaknesses in judgment, discernment and understanding. If a transgressor can humbly do this, these steps—in time—will create a move toward mutual attempts at healing as both parties try to help and heal each other. It should be repeated that the transgressor must, however, be willing to concede that he lacks righteous judgment and discernment at this time in his life in order for this to happen.

Relationships with children will have to be rebuilt and re-established, as well. A transgressor *must* see and acknowledge where his actions have been controlling and manipulative of these precious souls. Though the tendency to treat children with blame, impatience, anger and condemnation will not easily be overcome, these attempts must be made—with the added willingness of the transgressor to let go of a quick reaction and harsh judgments when he sees problems or the need for discipline. A transgressor needs to understand he does not have enough of the Spirit to discern adequately what would be best for these children, but that discernment will come through time and through patience as the influence of the Lord is allowed more strongly into his life. Often the insights of his wife will be needed to help him see how to effectively deal with situations where punishment or corrective action is necessary.

Earning Back Trust

Another essential step of the transgressor is the necessity of understanding that he must begin to earn back the trust that he has destroyed by his sins, lies and deception. A transgressor cannot expect or demand the innate trust that may have existed before to suddenly be back in relationships solely because he has begun the road to repentance. He must understand that his efforts, motives and behaviors will be questioned and distrusted for a lengthy period of time. Trust will not just re-establish itself in a relationship even if a transgressor feels—or insists—it should be there. A transgressor will have to earn it back effort by effort and step by step. Efforts will have to continue unceasingly and continuously until trust is a natural by-product of consistent action.

The Lord gave strict laws of restitution to the children of Israel that could serve as a guide in this way. Many times they would have to restore "double" or four to five times what they took or destroyed (see Exodus 22). For *every* behavior or misdeed of the past, then, there should be "double" or four to five righteous acts to restore what has been taken away.

Such things as consistently coming home from work on time; helping around the house more; being kind and patient to children even when whiney or complaining; handling situations with "gentleness and meekness, and by love unfeigned" (D&C 121:41) when interacting with anyone—including those outside the home; incorporating consistent efforts of spirituality; giving acts of service; and speaking with love and appreciation to those who have been hurt are some of the ways trust can begin to be re-developed.

As with the children of Israel,

> If they shall confess their iniquity, and the iniquity of their fathers, with their trespass which they trespassed against them, and that also they have walked contrary unto me;
>
> And *that* I also have walked contrary unto them; . . .if then their uncircumcised hearts be humbled, and they then accept of the punishment of their iniquity:
>
> Then will I remember my covenant with Jacob, and also my covenant with Isaac, and also my covenant with Abraham will I remember." (Leviticus 26:40-42)

When Church Action is Taken Against a Transgressor

Many times a transgressor will be disciplined through priesthood leaders for his transgressions in hopes that he will be able to see the seriousness and destruction of past sins and indiscretions. In order for healing to continue beyond the point of discipline, a transgressor must see this action as a step toward cleansing and wholeness, not as harsh judgment of priesthood leaders making the decisions regarding his worthiness. Anger or resentment at the ones rendering decisions will only cause a swift and rapid decline in the healing process—or perhaps stop it permanently. A transgressor must guard himself carefully against the feelings of anger and resentment that Satan will try to breed toward those called of the Lord to help and make these decisions.

Steven A. Cramer in his book *The Worth of a Soul* gives some great insights that can be used as a basis for viewing any type of church action. He said, "If one is to be successful in repenting and making his way back into the Church, he must be willing to pay the total price no matter what it costs in personal change and no matter how long it takes to make those improvements in character, spirit and behavior." (p. 55) Church action can often be the precursor that brings about these changes and improvements.

Church action, as necessary as it might be, brings about a sobering reality. As the Lord has said, "Verily, verily, I say unto you, if a man marry a wife according to my word, and they are sealed by the Holy Spirit of promise, according to mine appointment, and he or she shall commit any sin or transgression of the new and everlasting covenant whatever. . .they shall be destroyed in the flesh, and shall be delivered unto the buffetings of Satan unto the day of redemption." (D&C 132: 26) A transgressor must be aware that when he has sinned and violated marriage covenants, Satan will have the opportunity to buffet him—that is torment, persecute, afflict, hurt, cause him damage, etc. Hardships and trials must be expected—whether they come through physical difficulties, difficulties with work or other relationships, hardships, troubled emotions, etc. These are all a part of the consequences of sin. As it says in the *Doctrine & Covenants*, "Inasmuch as you are found transgressors, you cannot escape my wrath in your lives. Inasmuch as ye are cut off for transgression, ye cannot escape the buffetings of Satan until the day of redemption." (104:8-9)

Steven A. Cramer in *The Worth of a Soul* described the period of time during which he fell victim to Satan's buffetings. He writes:

> I suppose that these are merely words to a person who has never suffered through this type of experience, but these words send shivers of fear down my spine just remembering what the buffetings were like.
>
> . . .I was much like a puppet under the control of Satan's influence. . . From time to time I was inflicted with the most horrible emotions with no discernible cause. When these ferocious attacks came upon me, I would change in just a

few seconds from a normal rationality to a nearly
insane rage of bitterness and poison which was so
overwhelming that it almost choked me. Being so
suddenly filled with incomprehensible darkness
and evil emotions, I would find myself lashing out
with the vicious venom upon whoever was near,
which was usually my family, and most often my
wife. I now understand that my suffering was the
result of the torment of evil demons who constantly
surrounded and taunted me (see Hel. 13:37) but I
did not understand it then.

. . .This awful vulnerability to Satan's
buffetings hung over me like a constant dark
cloud. . . .Feeling like a rubber band stretched to
the breaking point, my emotions were constantly
tensed, just waiting and wondering when the next
attack would come. I might go for several weeks
without lapses, and then suddenly, like a whirlwind
and without warning, Satan would invade and
occupy again.

I know that I have not described this
experience adequately, but these are the only words
I can use to describe it. I have failed to communicate
the awful horror which we experienced, and my
heart aches for the thousands of families who are
now groping their way through their buffeting in
blindness as we did. (p. 70)

Steven Cramer then pleads with those working with
transgressors, "I plead with you, be kind and patient. Try to
reflect the unwavering love of the Lord for this person. This is
the only way you will be able to endure your own part in such
an experience, and your positive reaction and love may be the
only light [this person] can find in his penalty of darkness."
(Ibid., p. 71)

A Fatal Mistake: Attempting to Use Willpower Instead of

the Savior to Overcome Transgression

A mistake transgressors often make in attempts to overcome sin is trying to use *willpower* instead of admitting to *powerlessness* over an addiction and relying on the Savior to overcome it. This will completely stop any progression; transgression will inevitably reoccur. Willpower will *never* be strong enough to overcome transgression permanently. There may be periods of non-participation or moments of brief reform, but this will not last. There must be a complete change of heart brought about by our Savior. A. Dean Byrd and Mark D. Chamberlain describe it this way in their book, *Willpower is Not Enough*:

> We live in a time of unprecedented belief in human capacity.
> . . .Surely we can be captains of our fate!
> But, as we have seen, we are not—and when we try, we fail.
> Amidst the throngs shouting, "We can do it," "We're doing it," "We've done it," we need to interject our own rejoinder: "Thanks and glory be to God."
> We have prospered. We have many strengths and abilities. Does that mean we need God less now? Far from it. We are creatures; he is the creator. We are the clay; he is the potter. Whether we acknowledge it or not, we need God's help if we are to succeed in becoming like God.
> We were surprised when one client said his terrible struggles with self-control had actually, in a way, turned out to be a blessing. "I have always felt pretty self-sufficient. It took a problem like this to teach me that I couldn't do it alone."
> President Ezra Taft Benson has said, "Just as a man does not really desire food until he is hungry, so he does not desire the salvation of Christ until he knows why he needs Christ."
> Perhaps, then, if there is anything to be

learned from our struggles with willpower, it is that
we cannot do it on our own and we do need Christ.
Change does not come easily or quickly. But it is
possible when we rely on him. (p. 21)

Ammon in the *Book of Mormon* said it this way. "I know
I am nothing; as to my strength I am weak; therefore I will not
boast of myself, but I will boast of my God, for in his strength I
can do all things." (Alma 26:12)

Another man, Phil S., writes about this concept in the
following way in his book, *The Perfect Brightness of Hope:*

> The year following my excommunication
> was a pitiful scene. Living in my own disgrace, I
> would gather all of my willpower to try to stay
> sober, attend church, and earn the *right* to be
> forgiven. . . Memories of better times depressed me
> terribly. Stuck in the cycle of addiction, my guilt,
> fear, and the day-to-day problems of just living built
> up inside me until I drank again.
>
> . . .My drinking binges drove me back to AA
> [Alcoholics Anonymous]. Friends there preached
> the philosophy of "let go and let God." But I still
> stubbornly held to my philosophy that people who
> drank alcohol were weak-willed and evil. If all that
> was wrong with me was a weak will, I reasoned
> then, that more willpower was the answer. I could
> not comprehend the key paradox of the disease—*in
> admitting defeat lay the answer to winning.* Eluding me
> was the fact that spiritual power, the only medicine
> that can combat a *spiritual disease*, is set in motion
> by *surrender to God.* (p. 73)

This "surrender" occurred in the following experience:

> I hit bottom like a concrete slab plunging
> from the top of a twelve-story building. When I hit, I
> didn't even bounce—I just shattered. . . .Depression

rolled over me like the waves of a dark, stormy ocean. Heavy and suffocating, my condition was more than I could bear. There were no more tries left in me. I despaired. I prayed. My prayers were unlike any I had ever uttered. I didn't ask for anything. Not to stay sober. Not to have my job back. Not for my wife to stay. Not to remove my pain. Not for anything! I was conquered. All I could do was mutter words about my total and complete nothingness.

As my prayers continued, something about the way I viewed life began to alter. It was not as if I had been struck with sudden brilliance. I was not filled with the burnings of truth, or vivid testimony, or consummate peace. . . .It was just the opposite. Alcohol had won. I was broken. I knew I couldn't stay sober—no matter what. As this realization settled upon me, for the first time in my life, I honestly and completely gave my life over to a Power Greater than Myself. With childlike demeanor, I humbly asked for His protection and care. As a hopeless beggar, I surrendered all of me into the waiting arms of my Heavenly Father. *"Do with me what you will. I can do nothing with me."*

I began to feel a tiny stirring within me—a feeling of warmth, barely detectable, as if a penlight had been turned on in my bosom. An effectual key was turned. Somehow, I knew in my heart that it *could* be over. I stood at the crossroads that I had heard described in every AA meeting: "Half measures availed us nothing. We stood at the turning point. We asked His protection and care with complete abandon."

. . .I suddenly understood that if I could just focus my energy only *on today*, and turn the *guilt* of yesterday and the *fear* of tomorrow over to God, then this terrible ordeal could be over. Like finding and putting in place a long lost, last piece of a large jigsaw puzzle, the picture came clear. (p. 124)

He states in conjunction with this:

> I discovered through my experience that
> pride—self-will, willpower, selfishness—lies at
> the heart of addiction. Fed on pride, my selfish
> addictions grew out of control. But when I
> persistently surrendered my will to God, I was able
> to starve them to extinction.
> . . .As long as the addict believes that
> through his own power he can control the events
> and characters of his life, he will fail to overcome
> addiction. *Realizing that you are in a powerless
> situation must occur in order for you to feel the need
> to surrender to God.* This may happen through
> intervention or through personal awareness brought
> about by pain—*but it must happen.* (pp. 182-183,
> italics added)

One man, who finally came to this point of
"powerlessness," said he hurt so much and carried so much
internal agony from his sins that he was finally ready to risk
everything—even if necessary, the relationships with his
eternal family—to stop hiding his sins and become clean with
the Lord. This act became his first step toward healing—of
both him *and* his family.

Developing Spirituality

Another critical step in the healing process of a
transgressor is adopting the spiritual habits one has been so
lackadaisical and inconstant in before. Prayers must be said
morning and evening—at the very least; scriptures should
be read daily and consistently, not only for a few minutes
but for a half hour as a minimum; all church meetings should
be attended; and family attempts at spirituality should be
incorporated. As mentioned previously, increased spirituality
becomes the strongest and most effective key to fighting the
demons and temptations that have been so prevalent in a

transgressor's life.

Priesthood blessings should also be sought when a transgressor feels the need for extra protection and strength during times of battle, temptation, difficulty, buffeting and hardship. So often the Lord can express His tender love and confidence in the efforts of a transgressor through these special blessings. A humble approach to asking for blessings when one is in need can become a great tool in overcoming the darkness that has been pervasive in a transgressor's life.

Overcoming Step by Step

As shown from the points above, the overcoming of sin is a long step-by-step process that, no matter how great the determination and desire to move forward, will take much time, effort, energy, exertion and labor. It is time-consuming and exhausting. When a transgressor does not realize how demanding, arduous, difficult, and burdensome this task will be, he may open himself up to future sin or perhaps the discouragement and despair Satan would inflict on him to stop this process.

Discouragement and despair will become Satan's most powerful tools in attempts to stop healing. A transgressor must guard himself against these feelings, even when he slips temporarily. This despair and discouragement are often Satan's last-ditch efforts in holding on to a transgressor because he knows he will soon not have him in his grasp.

When caught in the web of despair and discouragement, powerful steps including intense prayer, fasting, priesthood blessings, putting one's name in the temple, increased scripture reading and so forth must be incorporated or serious damage may result. Sometimes wanting to give in completely to the sin becomes overpowering. Other times leaving home and family seems like the only option left. Some have even considered suicide to escape these overpowering feelings.

One transgressor had tried again and again to overcome his problems with pornography and did not feel like he was making any progress at all when he would fall back into his old patterns of behavior. As discouragement overcame him, he turned in desperation to thoughts of leaving this existence to escape what he felt was a trap of Satan he would never escape. He in essence told his wife, "Why should I stay here when I've caused so much damage to everyone and still cause damage, even when I'm trying hard to stop?" It took intense prayer, counseling and priesthood blessings to overcome this darkness and put him back on the road to recovery.

Another extremely damaging and cunning trick of Satan that leads to despair is Satan's attempts to convince a transgressor he has already committed the unpardonable sin. One man said, "I knew I had received promptings to confess and overcome my sins. Because of this knowledge, every time I kept falling, I kept feeling as if I had committed the 'unpardonable sin' by turning against the light I had received." Satan kept whispering this to him that this was the case. He had to come to trust that he had not become "lost forever" (Alma 42:6) before he could accept the help and mercy our Savior had to offer him.

Satan uses this "unpardonable sin" trap often to stop healing. Phil S. in *The Perfect Brightness of Hope* described a similar situation. He said:

> I knew that God forgave *others*. But I was sure my sins were extraordinary. *I seriously doubted I could be forgiven*. I even questioned whether I had committed the unpardonable sin, *denying the sun at noonday*, or in other words, forsaking Jesus Christ after having received a special testimony of His divinity. (p. 71)

Discouraging and despairing thoughts like these must be fought as powerfully as unclean thoughts and behaviors need to be. As said before, these thoughts are Satan's efforts to hold on to a transgressor and he many times succeeds in this.

Great spiritual efforts should be incorporated to overcome and free a transgressor from these binding traps.

> Yea, come unto Christ, and be perfected in him, and deny yourselves of all ungodliness; and if ye shall deny yourselves of all ungodliness, and love God with all your might, mind and strength, then is his grace sufficient for you, that by his grace ye may be perfect in Christ; and if by the grace of God ye are perfect in Christ, ye can nowise deny the power of God.
>
> And again, if ye by the grace of God are perfect in Christ, and deny not his power, then are ye sanctified in Christ by the grace of God, through the shedding of the blood of Christ, which is in the covenant of the Father unto the remission of your sins, that ye become holy, without spot. (Moroni 10:32-33)

A Lifetime Vulnerability

A person who has struggled with pornography addiction needs to understand that "recovery" from the addiction is much like recovery from alcoholism. As Phil S. quoted in *The Perfect Brightness of Hope*, alcoholism is a "disease that can be arrested *but not cured*. . . .For all. . .addicts, the only effective treatment is complete abstinence throughout the rest of his or her life. *At no point can the addict begin again. . .without falling swiftly back into uncontrollable addiction*." (p. 186)

Such is true of pornography addiction. Recovery doesn't mean one will develop complete immunity to the desire for pornography. It means one previously addicted to it, knowing his previous powerlessness over it, adopts behaviors and attitudes that keep him completely away from it. He avoids earlier thought patterns and behaviors that make him "drift" toward participation. Vigilance will always be needed throughout the rest of his life to guard him against participation. But, as one woman said, "So many previous transgressors turn out to be deeply spiritual men. They know their tendencies and weaknesses so they often have to try harder."

> Wherefore gird up the loins of your mind, be sober, and hope to the end for the grace that is to be brought unto you at the revelation of Jesus Christ;
>
> As obedient children, not fashioning yourselves according to the former lusts in your ignorance:
>
> But as he which has called you is holy, so be ye holy. (1st Peter 1:13-15)

7

Working With a Transgressor

Wives dealing with transgressors need to understand that for a great deal of time they will carry the greater burden of healing a relationship scarred by the use of pornography. This is not an easy responsibility to accept. These women are called upon to reach out and help transgressors who have hurt and betrayed them deeply. While struggling with intense wounds of their own, they are called upon to help those who will not see the "gross error" of their ways for a long time. (Moroni 8:6) There will be days of uncertainty and trial that will make these women wonder if a transgressor will ever overcome and become clean again—or let go of the anger, blame, manipulation and control that becomes so ingrained in a personality when sin has been present. It is only with the Savior that they make it through these uncertain days of trial and challenge to move toward healing.

Jeffrey R. Holland, in speaking to mothers, gave a powerful message that can apply in this instance. He said:

You can't possibly do this alone, but you do have help. The Master of Heaven and Earth is there to bless you—He who resolutely goes after the lost sheep, sweeps thoroughly to find the lost coin, waits everlastingly for the return of the prodigal son. Yours is the work of salvation, and therefore you will be magnified, compensated, made more than you are and better than you have ever been as you try to make honest effort, however feeble you may sometimes feel that to be.

Rely on Him. Rely on Him heavily. Rely on Him forever and "press forward with a steadfastness in Christ, having a perfect brightness of hope." (2nd Nephi 31:20) You are doing God's work. You are doing it wonderfully well. He is blessing you and he will bless you, even—no, *especially*—when your days and nights may be the most challenging. (*Ensign*, May 1997, p. 35)

One woman spoke of an experience she had as she worked with her husband who had been involved in sin. One night she fell to knees in prayer, weary and exhausted over having to deal with him—especially the anger and contention that continually came from him despite her efforts to work through their problems. She said in exasperation to the Lord that night, "I'm so tired. I'm done. I can't do this anymore." The Lord's gently chastising rejoinder came immediately to her mind. He said, "After all that I've done for you?" She knew through this admonition that He had called upon her to carry these burdens for Him, despite how difficult they had come to be for her. He wanted and asked her to carry these burdens for Him.

Those who are willing to do this type of work, however, will become closer and more aligned with the Savior than ever before as they learn to adopt His needed attributes of forgiveness, love and patience. This is not to say that the task will be easy and the road smooth. But those working hand in hand with the Savior will walk this difficult and arduous path with greater spiritual insight, direction and blessings than they've ever received previously. As with the Jaredites walking into the wilderness where "there never had man been, . . .the Lord [will] go before them. . .and g(i)ve directions whither they should travel." (Ether 2:5)

During times of struggle and uncertainty, gifts of charity, long-suffering, patience and understanding will often be given them from the Lord. Sometimes these blessings are poured out abundantly, as if coming from a free-flowing conduit from heaven, helping them fill the empty, drained buckets that will be theirs because of their daily strugglings. When reaching an unknown juncture or when difficulties, trials and challenges arise—often daily or hourly, answers, insight, direction and peace many times come swiftly and clearly just for the asking.

It must be stressed that this learning to forgive and act like the Savior is an ongoing process. Since we are all imperfect people struggling to find the right path toward salvation, this learning will come in gradual, progressive steps—much like the process needed for a transgressor in overcoming sin. But spiritual blessings will come freely and consistently to those who strive in patience and faith to deal with the unrighteous actions of another the Savior's way.

The Zion of Enoch was surrounded by wickedness, but "Enoch and all his people walked with God, and he dwelt in the midst of Zion." (Moses 7:69) So, too, can the Lord walk with those working with transgressors and shield them from the evils surrounding them. As He has said in the scriptures, "I will go before your face. I will be on your right hand and on your left, and my Spirit shall be in your hearts, and mine angels round about you, to bear you up." (D&C 84:88) When one is willing to find and do the Lord's will in working with a transgressor, this becomes an enduring, eternal promise that will help that person through the difficulties, challenges and trials that invariably come. The Lord will be in front of them as an example and light; beside them offering strength and comfort; and behind them whispering words of guidance and direction. This is His eternal mission and His promises are sure. (Alma 37:17)

Repentance Can't be Forced or Coerced

One truly difficult concept for injured parties to face and accept is that transgressors cannot be forced, coerced or prodded into repentance. They cannot be made to see the deep wounds of betrayal, hurt and internal injuries they have caused. They cannot be compelled to admit behaviors, traits and actions that have been off base and detrimental to themselves and others. It is only through the Spirit—and time—that transgressors will come to see realities and past truths—and the need for deep, ongoing repentance. In other words, injured partners can never work out the salvation of their partners, no matter how much they wish or desire to do so. It is only the Savior who can.

This is not to say those injured parties cannot persuade, reason with, exhort, entreat and admonish their partners toward better behaviors and repentance. It is to say that these injured parties cannot control the repentance process or move it forward on their own timing. Satan often tries to convince them that they can. He gets his clutches around them when he convinces them that unless they are endlessly threatening, prodding, pushing and reminding their spouses about what must be done, what must be changed and what must be acknowledged in terms of past mistakes, they are denying the problems that exist in their lives and marriages.

Trying to control behavior like this can be seen as "co-dependent" behavior which Phil S. effectively describes in *The Perfect Brightness of Hope*:

> Addiction is a family disease. Those individuals who live closest to the addict are affected the most. The term "co-dependent" refers to these individuals, usually a parent, spouse, child,

or friend, who are living in a close relationship with an addict. The co-dependent's behavior becomes intertwined or dependent on the behavior of the addicted person. These individuals attempt to control the irrational behavior of the addict. Unable to do so, they begin to believe they—the co-dependents—are to blame. Unable to separate their own emotions from the addict's, co-dependents feel the addict's hurt, fear, guilt, and pain. They, too, become emotionally ill as they take on ever-increasing worries and fears about important family issues that the addict neglects.

. . .Over a short period, a co-dependent's mood can swing from anger, to resentment, to guilt, to anxiety, to elation, to despair, all based upon the behavior of the addict. Ultimately, co-dependents become so fixated on the other's behavior, they lose their own identity. They spiral downward, deeper into their own emotion and physical illness. And, just like the addict, they deny their own illness.

. . .The flaw in co-dependents' thinking is that they have centered all of their attention on the *addict's behavior* and trying to control him. In doing this, they lose sight of what they *can* control. This paradigm can only be remedied when a co-dependent shifts his thinking focus from outward—what he can't control, the addict's behavior—to inward—what he has some control over, himself. The co-dependent must come to realize that, in order to save himself, he has to stop focusing on and trying to control the addict. If he doesn't, his own future is at terrible risk. (pp. 187-189)

As the scriptures say,

No power or influence can or ought to be maintained by virtue of the priesthood, only by persuasion, by long-suffering, by gentleness and meekness, and by love unfeigned;

By kindness and pure knowledge, which shall greatly enlarge the soul without hypocrisy, and without guile—

Reproving betimes with sharpness, when moved upon by the Holy Ghost; and then showing forth afterwards an increase of love toward him whom thou hast reproved, lest he esteem thee to be his enemy;

That he may know that thy faithfulness is stronger than the cords of death. (D&C 121:41-44)

Confusing "Forgiveness" with Allowing Evil Behaviors to Continue

There is a fine line between forgiveness and allowing evil behaviors to continue unabated in a home. Slip-ups of sin, contention or other problems brought in by a transgressor should only be allowed insofar as a transgressor is willing to repent and make restitution for these mistakes. "If he confess his sins before thee and me, and repenteth in the sincerity of his heart, him shall ye forgive, and I will forgive him also," Mosiah 26:29 states. Evil behaviors must and should not be allowed indefinitely, however. As with the Nephites, "(The Lord) will not suffer you that ye shall live in your iniquities, to destroy his people." (Alma 9:19)

Lili De Hoyos Anderson, a marriage and family counselor, during one group session made some strong, valid points about victims of sin not becoming "enablers"—those people who allow sin to go on unstopped and unchecked in a home without making any efforts to heal or overcome. When victims look upon sin with "continual allowance" like this, they "subsidize the destruction of the sinner," she claims. "Victims must set boundaries, for there is a limit to what one must bear."

She then said, "Do not be victimized to the point

that you stop your progression—your 'ascent' to the celestial kingdom. God does not want us to be victims. Victims will continue their stay in the 'telestial realm' with a transgressor when allowing sins to go on unchanged."

She then quoted James E. Faust in the April, 1993, General Conference of the Church when he said:

> What might be "just cause" for the breaking the covenants of marriage? Over a lifetime of dealing with human problems, I have struggled to understand what might be considered "just cause" for breaking of covenants. I confess I do not claim the wisdom nor authority to definitively state what is "just cause." Only the parties to the marriage can determine this. They must bear the responsibility for the train of consequences which inevitably follow if these covenants are not honored. In my opinion, "just cause" should be nothing less serious than a prolonged and apparently irredeemable relationship which is destructive of a person's dignity as a human being. (*Ensign*, May 1993, p. 36)

There are gospel-inspired boundaries set in a marriage, she continued. These include not allowing such things as adultery, homosexuality, abuse of any kind, addictions of any kind, or anything that is "grossly destructive." When these are allowed and a blind eye is turned, destruction snowballs and the enabler becomes a part of it.

The Lord has counseled us, "Verily I say unto you, if that enemy shall escape my vengeance, that he be not brought into judgment before me, then *ye* shall see to it that ye warn him in my name, that he come no more upon you, neither upon your family." (D&C 98:28, italics added) It thus becomes the responsibility of the victim to make the first move toward cleansing. If a victim does not take responsibility, that person becomes a part of the problem.

This point can be illustrated in the following true

account. One woman and her sister-in-law basically discovered during a certain time frame that their husbands, both brothers, were struggling with addictions to pornography. The first woman became insistent that sin and transgression be cleansed from her home and from their lives; she refused to allow her husband's continuing choices without his suffering severe consequences in their relationship. Like she did with her children, she set "boundaries" for him that he could not cross.

But her sister-in-law basically became an "enabler" of her husband's sins. She in essence did nothing and continued to allow him his awful choices without insisting he stop or refrain from his harmful actions. She took his barrages of degradation, anger and resentment instead of insisting that he own up to the truth. She seldom fought back but fell victim to his bullying and disrespectful treatment of her.

These behaviors continued on unabated as her husband continued his sins. Finally, her husband chose to leave her, ultimately having an affair and fathering a child out of wedlock. The other woman, however, because of her insistence of righteousness in their home, became an instrument of healing in her marriage and family. Two opposite extremes happened because of the insistence of righteousness on one end and the allowance of sin on the other.

Another woman handled continuing sins in her marriage in the following way that moved them toward healing instead of making her an "enabler." Her husband, who had become addicted to pornography, had counseled with the Bishop and confessed his problems to her, but despite his efforts, his sins continued unchecked. The first time he "fell" after these steps, it was "horrible" for her. She shed many tears and felt much pain, heartache and sorrow. The second time he fell was much the same. However, the third time she basically told him, in an abrupt, straightforward way, "If this happens again, I will never come back to you. I will no longer allow this in my life or in my home." When she took this step, he was finally able to move beyond unstopped relapses of participation and begin true healing in their relationship.

The Lord has said,

> Were it not for the transgressions of my people, speaking concerning the church and not individuals, they might have been redeemed even now.
>
> But they have not learned to be obedient to the things which I required at their hands, but are full of all manner of evil.
>
> . . .Zion cannot be built up unless it is by the principles of the law of the celestial kingdom; otherwise I cannot receive her unto myself.
>
> And my people must needs be chastened until they learn obedience, if it must needs be, by the things which they suffer. (D&C105:2-3; 5-6)

Suffering sometimes means not removing "the natural consequences of an addict's behavior," Phil S. wrote in *The Perfect Brightness of Hope*.

> This is a crucial principle to understand: *The more we remove the natural consequences of addictive behavior from our loved ones and friends, the more we ensure that they will remain irresponsible and unable to recognize their need for help.* . . . Accumulative physical and emotional pain. . .forces the addict toward a solution. *Don't take away their pain!* They will eventually respond. In the Old Timer's words, "We are just sick and tired of being sick and tired." Although I experienced numerous treatment programs, pain still got my attention best. Somewhere within myself, I understood that I had to suffer the consequences of my choices in order to learn to not make those choices. I even reached a point where I gave explicit instructions to those who were consistently helping me avoid consequences— to stop! (p. 179)

Forgiveness Even When a Relationship is Not Healed

Often a transgressor has become so entrenched in sin and transgression that he will not be able to make his way out in time to heal a marriage and family. As it says in 2 Timothy 4:10, he "hath forsaken me, having loved this present world." It should be understood that if this occurs, forgiveness of the transgressor is still essential for the one injured or that person will never overcome the past but will always carry lasting emotional scars.

This person must turn the transgressor and past injuries over to the Lord trusting that "judgment is mine. . .and vengeance is mine, . . .and I will repay." (Mormon 8:20) The Lord will make all necessary reparations and judgments in the future; it is not necessary but damaging for the injured party to try to do so. The Lord commands us to leave justice and retribution up to Him. Only He can take on the responsibility of judging those who have transgressed. When we take it upon ourselves, we only hurt and hinder our own progress. We must follow His counsel when he says, "hold on thy way" and "fear not what man can do, for God shall be with you forever and ever." (D&C 122:9)

Remember, however, that the process of forgiving transgressors who have hurt and wounded innocent parties and devastated their lives is a process much like the process of moving toward perfection. It is never easy and will take time, tears, prayer, effort, patience and faith in a Being whose "ways are higher than your ways," and whose thoughts are higher "than your thoughts." (Isaiah 55:9) It is only the Lord who will help someone reach this level of forgiveness; this forgiveness will ultimately come as a gift from Him to someone sincerely striving to do His will.

Forgiveness: A Necessary Protection

Forgiveness is truly a necessary protection for those who have been wronged and is an essential part of the Lord's plan of salvation, whether or not a transgressor stays in or leaves a marriage. The Lord has said, "Wherefore, I say unto you, that ye ought to forgive one another; for he that forgiveth not his brother his trespasses standeth condemned before the Lord; *for there remaineth in him the greater sin.*" (D&C 64:9, italics added) When viewed in this light, it is scary and frightening for those not forgiving transgressors. It is as if having the transgressors' sins plus *more* sins placed upon their shoulders. Think of the darkness, evil, buffetings and onslaughts from the adversary that this can engender.

These are real and frightening truths. One woman felt these powers of darkness as she learned about the grievous sins of her husband, who had, unbeknownst to her, been involved extensively in pornography throughout their married life. In the first several trying days after his confession—when she still blamed, despised and felt intense anger for his deceptive actions—she felt the influence and powers of these spirits in her home. "They were powerful and overwhelming," she said. "I became subject to their darkness during this time because of my inability to even attempt to forgive [my husband] or soften my heart in any way. I felt their destructive influence and their hatred for me and my family. They literally tormented me. They would plant again and again in my mind visual images of the sins my husband had been involved in that became devastating to me and filled me with a deep sense of betrayal and pain.

"When I was finally able to get over the initial emotion and begin to try and forgive my husband with the Savior's help, I felt the power and grasp of these spirits begin to dissipate. With my continuing efforts of earnest prayer to garner needed strength to fight them in this way, I soon gained more power over them. I've never felt as deeply the need for each of us to forgive others, especially transgressors. We cannot afford to become subject to the spirits that have tormented and plagued them."

For one woman, the idea of not forgiving could ultimately be seen by her as a denial of the atonement of our Savior. She said, "The Lord has told us all that He can and will

forgive all sins except the unpardonable sin of denying the Holy
Ghost. That would include my husband's sins. He has also told
us that He can heal our hurts, wounds and injuries. That would
include my hurts, wounds and injuries. When I first struggled
terribly to try to forgive my husband because I couldn't get over
my injuries and pain, I slowly began to understand that if I
didn't believe what the Savior had said, I would always be filled
with terrible pain and never be able to move forward. I learned
to trust that the Lord could truly heal the two of us—either
independently, if our marriage did not work out, or together—
if we both tried to turn to Him.

"When I finally learned to turn more completely to the
Lord, trusting He would eventually heal me from my pain,
then I could finally give my husband and his sins to Him, too,
trusting that He could eventually heal him. I learned I wasn't
the one that had to make it all right, and I could—and had
to—draw upon the powers of the atonement for the strength I
needed to move on with my life."

Forgiveness by the injured party is an essential part of
healing, but it should be noted once again that this is a long
process that requires the help and sustaining power of the Lord.
There will be steps forward and steps backward in a cyclical
pattern of moving successively upward. One should accept
these backward steps as part of the process, and in turn be able
to apply the same amount of forgiveness to oneself when faced
with the inability to forgive immediately and completely. It is
a process that requires time, effort and the sustaining power of
the Savior to achieve.

One woman, after she had stumbled intensely in her
forgiveness of her husband, found these scriptures in the *New
Testament* that helped her move forward once again:

> Let us hold fast the profession of *our* faith
> without wavering;
> . . .And let us consider one another to
> provoke unto love and good works:

. . .Vengeance *belongeth* unto me, I will recompense, saith the Lord. And again, The Lord shall judge His people.

. . .Call to remembrance the former days, in which, after ye were illuminated, ye endured a great fight of afflictions.

. . .Cast not away therefore your confidence, which hath great recompense of reward. . .

For ye have need of patience, that, after ye have done the will of the Lord, ye might receive the promise. (Hebrews 10:23-24; 30; 32; 35-36)

There's a final strong admonition pertaining to forgiveness that needs to be made at this point. An injured party needs to forgive *the Lord* for allowing difficult circumstances and trials into their lives. One of Satan's powerful tools is anger toward God for putting innocent parties in difficult situations.

Not only have we often made covenants with the Lord before this life to bear these heavy burdens, anger will turn us against the only source of true healing and comfort that we can find amidst our afflictions. We cannot afford to harbor bitterness against the Lord but must "remember, remember that it is not the work of God that is frustrated, but the work of men." (D&C 3:3) We must understand it is not God who has caused these trials in our lives but the evil choices of men misusing their gifts of agency.

"For although a man may have many revelations, and have power to do many mighty works, yet if he boasts in his own strength, and sets at naught the counsels of God, *and follows after the dictates of his own will and carnal desires, he must fall and incur the vengeance of a just God upon him.*" (D&C 3: 4, italics added) This fall is what affects the innocent parties surrounding a transgressor—not the Lord's will for them. The Lord desires and wants their wholeness, happiness and well-being.

When a Transgressor Can Begin to Trust in a Spouse's Forgiveness

When a transgressor can truly begin to trust that a spouse will honestly try to forgive him for his past sins and indiscretions when he is sincerely striving to repent, the process of healing a relationship will escalate dramatically. We can learn a great lesson from the Savior in this regard. We all know and can rest assured that the Lord will forgive us when we come unto Him in humility and with a contrite heart. As He has said, "I, the Lord, forgive sins unto those who confess their sins before me and ask forgiveness, who have not sinned unto death." (D&C 64:7)

When a transgressor can develop trust similar to this in a partner, this partner can truly become an instrument of healing in the Lord's hands. *This is not to say a wife must silently put up with continuing, unabated sins or with an unrepentant transgressor who won't or does not desire to change.* This idea applies to transgressors who are trying to overcome sins in a humble, submissive way, even if they do stumble occasionally. A forgiving spouse can be a tremendous asset to future growth and healing.

Forgiveness Even When a Transgressor's Behavior is Contentious

A transgressor struggling to overcome sin will many times become angry and contentious, blaming others on the outside for his problems or difficulties—especially a wife. Irony lies in the fact that when a transgressor often needs the most help, he will most likely be the most contentious and angry toward a partner, pushing away efforts of reconciliation or problem-solving. Control and manipulation through aggression or anger is often used instead of calm reasoning or working through issues.

Forgiveness for even these kinds of behaviors is necessary for a relationship to heal, despite how difficult it is to do this. As one Bishop said, "Unsanctified behavior on the part of the husband does not justify unsanctified behavior on the part of the wife." In other words, wrong choices of one do not justify wrong choices of another. Severe and sometimes irreparable damage can occur when both parties become angry and contentious.

It should be strongly noted here that forgiveness for contention from a transgressor does not mean lying down and taking the barbs, attacks, blame, unleashed aggression and contention that comes; it does mean not returning these in revenge or in attempts to wound or hurt back. Elder David E. Sorensen said it like this:

> I would like to make it clear that forgiveness of sins should not be confused with tolerating evil. The Savior asks us to forsake and combat evil in all its forms, and although we must forgive a neighbor who injures us, we should still work constructively to prevent that injury from being repeated. A woman who is abused should not seek revenge, but neither should she feel that she cannot take steps to prevent further abuse. A businessperson treated unfairly in a transaction should not hate the person who was dishonest but could take appropriate steps to remedy the wrong. *Forgiveness does not require us to accept or tolerate evil. It does not require us to ignore the wrong that we see in the world around us or in our lives.* But as we fight against sin, we must not allow hatred or anger to control our thoughts and actions. (*Ensign*, May 2003, p. 12, italics added)

Oftentimes in order to do this a partner must leave a situation where there is unrestrained venom so as not to cause further damage. Sometimes demanding third-party involvement to work through issues is essential, as well. This means, in essence, discussing difficulties with a Bishop or counselor as necessary. Sometimes a partner of a transgressor has to claim, "I can see we can't work this out together. There is too much anger, resentment and blame going on. I refuse to discuss this issue with you again unless there is a third party present to mediate so we don't cause further harm to me or our relationship."

Another issue to note is that many times during the repentance process, contentious issues will come up in regards to raising, punishing or disciplining children when dealing with them directly. One couple, who knew their predisposition toward contention when these issues arose in the home, had to choose a code word that would allow them to say, "The situation is becoming contentious. We need to speak privately before any further damage is done in front of or to the children." They would then escape to a room to discuss the issues that had arisen without further involving the children. Often behavior like this is desperately needed to safeguard the children from wounds and pain in seeing their parents bickering and fighting.

During times of contention, the Lord will help those working with transgressors know what to do. He has said, "Preach the word; be instant in season, out of season, reprove, rebuke, exhort with all longsuffering and doctrine." (2nd Timothy 4:2) Prayers similar to Alma's should ascend when doing this. Alma said, "O Lord, their souls are precious, and many of them are our brethren; therefore, give unto us, O Lord, power and wisdom that we may bring these, our brethren, again unto thee." (Alma 31:35) And, as Paul counsels in the *New Testament*:

> Thou therefore endure hardness as a good soldier of Jesus Christ.
> . . .The servant of the Lord must not strive; but be gentle unto all men, apt to teach, patient,
> In meekness instructing those that oppose themselves; if God peradventure will give them repentance to the acknowledging of the truth;
> And *that* they may recover themselves out of

the snare of the devil, who are taken captive by him
at his will. (2nd Timothy 2:3, 24-26)

Again, learning to apply patience and forgiveness for
the sins and weaknesses of others is a long, difficult process
and requires patience and forgiveness in equal amounts for the
one striving to reach this point. Forgiving one's own contention
and anger while dealing with problems is as important as
forgiving a transgressor's anger and contention. Satan tries
many times to convince those who stumble and fall in their
efforts of forgiveness that the Lord's patience and mercy does
not apply to them because they haven't been perfect in their
responses and attitudes. This is untrue because "the tender
mercies of the Lord are over all those whom he hath chosen,
because of their faith, to make them mighty even unto the
power of deliverance." (1 Nephi 1:20) He will do this, despite
temporary setbacks.

It should be noted, too, that sternness and firmness
when dealing with contention should not be mistaken for
anger, even when a transgressor insists these behaviors are
contentious. Holding firmly to one's own opinions or ideas in
the face of opposition is a necessary part of working through
the problems that will arise because of sin. Often transgressors
will try to blame those who do this, saying they are unwilling
to work through issues—or that their partners are emotionally
unhealthy or controlling. This is not the case. It is not wrong
but necessary to hold on firmly to what one believes is right
when working through difficult issues.

Developing Patience for Dealing with Continued
Weaknesses of a Transgressor

One woman had some experiences that helped her
gain insight into the patience she would need in helping her
husband overcome his addictive tendencies. During the year
before she found out about her husband's sinful behavior, she
went through some tremendous physical trials which resulted

in two surgeries and months and months of healing. During this time, she struggled with fatigue, depression and pain. She could hardly function and felt emotionally drained and weary. Increased weight became the most troublesome issue for her, but she scarcely had the time to exercise or do anything else about it and felt increasingly discouraged about her condition.

When the sinful actions of her husband came to light, she realized through an impression in her mind that the Lord had given her all of those previous physical difficulties—especially the inability to lose weight—so she could relate, in a small way, to what it would be like for her husband to overcome his sins. She knew and sensed the hardship of it because she had tasted some of her own. This experience gave her added capacity to try to garner the patience she would need to deal with the difficulties that would arise in their marriage during her husband's attempts to overcome his transgressions.

For those needing patience to deal with transgressors' weaknesses in this way, prayers should be offered similar to Alma's when he prayed regarding the wicked Zoramites. "O Lord God," he said,

> wilt thou give me strength, that I may bear with mine infirmities. For I am infirm, and such wickedness among this people doth pain my soul.
> O Lord, my heart is exceedingly sorrowful; wilt thou comfort my soul in Christ. O Lord, wilt thou grant unto me that I may have strength, *that I may suffer with patience these afflictions which shall come upon me*, because of the iniquity of this people. (Alma 31:30-31, italics added)

By adopting this attitude of patience, those working with transgressors can become instrumental in helping transgressors discover needed keys and tools for overcoming sin. They can be messengers of the promise that the Lord "is just in all his works, and that he has all power to save *every man* that believeth on his name and bringeth forth fruit meet for repentance." (Alma 12:15, italics added)

Giving Unconditional Love

Unconditional love for a transgressor can be demonstrated by an injured party in two important ways that become conducive to healing a damaged relationship. The first way is what could be termed "not manipulating a transgressor's humility." In other words, when a transgressor becomes humble and willing to listen to faults and errors or discuss problems in a good way without fighting or contending back, this time should never be used by a partner to blame, criticize, chastise relentlessly, judge, or spew unabated anger, resentment and animosity. As the scriptures say, "Condemn me not because of mine imperfection. . .but rather give thanks unto God that he hath made manifest unto you [my] imperfections, that ye may learn to be more wise than [I] have been." (Mormon 9:31)

This is not to say that honest, open, non-condemning concerns about behaviors can't be expressed or discussed. It is to say this should be done in an enlightening way, where a discussion is used as a tool to help a transgressor overcome sin, not where a transgressor is trodden down relentlessly by past mistakes. The Lord said, "Fools mock, but they shall mourn; and my grace is sufficient for the meek, that *they shall take no advantage of thy weakness*." (Ether 12:26, italics added) As the Prophet Joseph Smith stated:

> You need not be teasing your husbands because of their deeds, but let the weight of your innocence, kindness and affection be felt, which is more mighty than a millstone hung about the neck; not war, not jangle, not contradiction, or dispute, but meekness, love, purity—these are the things that should magnify you in the eyes of all good men. (*Teachings*, p. 227)

Times to teach and help a transgressor will come during occasional "teaching moments" when a transgressor is either humble or despairing—and thus ready to listen. Satan's biggest tool in an injured party's life is to have that person use unabated anger and resentment during these times instead of using these moments for encouragement and strengthening. If one injured approaches these times with humility, however, that person can truly become the Lord's mouthpiece and offer His words of counsel and comfort to the transgressor.

It should be noted that feelings of anger, hurt, pain, resentment and bitterness on the part of those who have been injured by transgressors are normal reactions to sinful behavior. Those feelings will need to be expressed, worked through and overcome, as well, during times when contention is absent. But there is a fine balance between expressing these feelings and honestly trying to work through them or using these feelings to strike back, wound or get revenge. The tenuous balance of discussing difficult issues without manipulation and damaging contention will only be found through extreme effort, patience and unceasing work—and after many, many setbacks. But this balance can and will be found by those couples sincerely trying to heal their relationship with the Savior's help.

One couple's relationship changed dramatically when a transgressor, in his despairing moments after participation in sin, received a letter from his wife asserting her love and faith in him as a person. She affirmed her willingness and desire to work with him and her knowledge that he was an incredible spiritual man with tremendous capacities. This gesture helped their marriage turn the corner and resulted in this transgressor ultimately desiring to clean up his life so that they could become a family once again.

Another couple's relationship turned toward healing when a wife had intended to say, "Think of how much pain you've caused me," but instead felt impressed to say, "*You* must have felt so much pain going through this." This statement opened up the transgressor's heart and he shared openly with her afterward, providing a turning point in their relationship.

Another way an injured spouse can help show unconditional love that can move a relationship toward healing is by not withholding much-needed gestures of love toward the transgressor. Not only do these gestures include kindness that is shown through service and action, it includes physical intimacy. Intimacy during attempts at healing can become a powerful tool to help transgressors heal and overcome the past. This does not mean to infer it will always be easy or desirous for an injured party to open up in this way. In fact, it is often difficult and hurtful, making one feel extremely vulnerable. Powerful prayers that the Lord will help and sustain them during these times need to ascend heavenward so intimacy does not become damaging, as it may have been before, but a tool for healing and growing closeness.

Steven A. Cramer's wife in *The Worth of a Soul* shared a letter with her parents that showed the struggle she went through during the first act of intimacy after her husband's confessions of sin. She wrote:

> All my married life I've thought that if my husband was ever unfaithful to me, the marriage would end, and justly so. I knew I'd never be able to make love to him again, and I felt divorce would be the only right answer. But all I could think of then was that Heavenly Father still loves (my husband] and that we are commanded to forgive every man his trespasses. I was hurting so badly that all I wanted to do was turn to God, who loves me, and do as I thought He wanted me to do, for I knew I could obtain surcease from pain and feel peace in only that way. Heavenly Father blessed me that my love for Steven didn't die. I knew that if he was truly repentant and willing to pay the price, my duty was to stick by him.
>
> . . .I want to tell you one more thing about this, and I hope you won't be offended by the

intimacy of it. After the Bishop left and our course was set, I realized my lot was cast with my husband's. He said he'd give me all the time I needed before we made love again, but the time came sooner than I expected. He didn't insist, but I knew what he felt and that he wanted to make things right between us. I struggled with myself: "Should I give in so quickly? Shouldn't he be made to wait longer? It's not fair that he sins like that and then expects me to welcome him right back! He needs some kind of disciplinary action from me, doesn't he?" But that's not forgiveness, is it? The scriptures say, "Vengeance is mine." If that is true, then God will mete out the punishment more justly and fairly than I could, and I wouldn't have to worry about it at all. Forgiveness means no grudge, no recriminations, no withholding love. And so I came to a decision. In my mind I said, "Dear Lord, the burden is yours. I forgive him totally and completely, and all the rest remains with you."

. . .It was almost physical—that transference of me to Christ of the hurt feelings and fear and even self-righteousness I'd been feeling. For the first time in my life I have come to truly appreciate and understand what His atonement means to me!

I'm not naive enough to think it is going to be easy, for I know there will be some very trying times ahead. And I'm not saintly enough to keep the sordid aspects of it continually at bay in my mind. Christ didn't promise an easy time—just that His burden and His yoke are easier and lighter than any we might choose for ourselves. (pp. 37-38)

Her efforts and Christ-like love were later attributed by her husband as key factors that ultimately healed their damaged relationship and marriage.

One struggling physically to love a husband after he has been unfaithful can rest assured in the knowledge that the Lord will sustain, bless and heal one who reaches to Him for help during times of intimacy. As one woman had been told in a blessing after her husband's unfaithfulness, "Offer yourself to him." When she tried to do this with physical intimacy, she always felt emotionally and spiritually sustained instead of depleted, used and drained, as she'd imagined she would feel after his betrayal.

As shown from the above examples, unconditional love becomes essential in working with transgressors. Those parties doing so should pray mightily for the strength and capacity to have charity, for

> charity suffereth long, and is kind, and envieth not, and is not puffed up, seeketh not her own, is not easily provoked, thinketh no evil, and rejoiceth not in iniquity but rejoiceth in the truth, beareth all things, believeth all things, hopeth all things, endureth all things.
>
> . . .Charity never faileth. Wherefore, cleave unto charity, which is the greatest gift of all, for all things must fail—
>
> But charity is the pure love of Christ, and it endureth forever; and whoso is found possessed of it at the last day, it shall be well with him.
>
> . . .Pray unto the Father with all the energy of heart, that ye may be filled with this love, which he hath bestowed upon all who are the true followers of his Son, Jesus Christ. (Moroni 7:45-48)

With this charity, great blessings may come to transgressors, "For unto such shall ye continue to minister; for ye know not but what they will return and repent, and come unto me with full purpose of heart, and I shall heal them; *and ye shall be the means of bringing salvation unto them.*" (3 Nephi 18:32, italics added)

Moving Forward

As shown from the above examples, the wife of a transgressor truly comes to bear the greater portion of healing in the initial stages of overcoming transgression. As shown too, however, the Lord is anxious to walk with those whose wills are aligned with His. He will accept of the burdens laid at His feet and will grant that those "burdens may be light." (Alma 33:23) The Lord's strength can thus become the strength of those who are striving to overcome the consequences of others' sins.

He promises in the *Doctrine & Covenants*:

> I, the Lord, am merciful and gracious unto those who fear me, and delight to honor those who serve me in righteousness and truth unto the end.
>
> Great shall be their reward and eternal shall be their glory.
>
> To them will I reveal all mysteries of my kingdom. . .and for ages to come, will I make known unto them the good pleasure of my will concerning all things pertaining to my kingdom.
>
> Yea, even the wonders of eternity shall they know, and things to come will I show them, even the things of many generations.
>
> And their wisdom shall be great, and their understanding reach to heaven; and before them the wisdom of the wise shall perish, and the understanding of the prudent shall come to naught.
>
> For by my Spirit will I enlighten them, and by my power will I make known unto them the secrets of my will. (76:5-10)

Ultimately and ideally, in a relationship where the Lord's charity and love is applied by those who have been injured, the transgressors in those relationships will eventually adopt the same characteristics and begin to reciprocate them back toward their partners—that is, if transgressors have chosen to repent. As transgressors move toward wholeness with the Savior's help, they then can become instruments of healing and strength for those they have harmed. This will *never* happen initially, however, but only comes about after those injured make the first moves toward healing and wholeness with the Savior's help.

8
Rebuilding Damaged Relationships

As shown in previous chapters, repairing a relationship after there has been a pornography addiction is a long, agonizing, painful process fraught with heartache, turmoil, confusion, anguish and suffering—on both sides. Where sacred, eternal marriage covenants have been broken, there exists a need for deep, inward healing in both partners. The time frame needed to heal and rebuild encompasses months and years, not days and weeks. There must be a complete starting over. The old relationship and covenants have become invalid through sin, and previous ways of relating will no longer work. In other words, the old relationship is dead. It must be rebuilt. As one marriage counselor told a couple whose lives had been broken by the husband's sexual addiction, "Because of what happened, your relationship has been destroyed. It is only through the grace of God that it will be rebuilt."

This process of rebuilding becomes as varied as each individual. One common factor that must be essential throughout the process, however, is that individuals and couples must surrender completely and thoroughly to the will of the Lord for them. If this does not happen, ultimate healing in the relationship will not occur. It is only through the Savior that couples will garner the strength, fortitude, insights and direction to move toward wholeness.

This process is symbolized by those people in Lehi's dream who were overcome by mists of terrible and overwhelming darkness. These people could see nothing on the path ahead and were saved only when they grasped tightly to the iron rod, never letting go. As they held on throughout the storms of darkness, not even knowing where they were placing their next steps, they were ultimately led to the light and life-giving joy of the Tree of Life. (1 Nephi 8:23-24)

Thus it can be with partners in a broken marriage relationship if *both* parties turn to the Savior and hold on tightly, with both hands, to that iron rod. The Savior can lead couples through the dark wilderness of sin, addiction, pain, betrayal, loss, heartache and mistrust toward the light of His healing love and wholeness. It has happened to many couples who have applied the Savior's atonement into their broken lives and marriages. As Mark H. Butler, an associate professor of Marriage and Family Therapy at Brigham Young University, observed:

> I have seen individuals and couples rise from the ashes of addiction—from sackcloth and ashes—to a newness of life. I have seen husbands and wives—with broken spirits and contrite hearts—humbly place their lives in the hands of God and meekly submit to his wisdom and will. I have seen a redemptive, healing power manifest in their personal lives and in their relationships. I have seen relationships lying, as it were, on their deathbeds like the youthful daughter of Jairus, only to be raised up and restored to life and hope and vitality. (KJB-Mark 5:22-24, 35-43.)
> I would not wish the devastation of addiction

on anyone. Gratefully, I have seen the power of God take this evil out of the lives of individuals, couples and families and in its stead raise up an individual, marriage, or family that was stronger, more unified, more undivided, more loyal, more covenanted and consecrated, and more like Christ. I have seen the horrible weaknesses of addiction forsaken and replaced by new strengths in both marriage and personal life. I can echo the words of Psalm 30:5, which says that "weeping may endure for a night, but joy cometh in the morning." Nevertheless, the journey is a long night of darkness." *(BYU Families Under Fire Conference, Oct. 3, 2002)*

The Long Journey of Healing

Though each couple's avenues of healing will vary, there are some general principles that can be incorporated that help with the process. They are as follows:

• *Finding the Necessary Balance of Forgiveness and Humility*

Both forgiveness and humility become the two essential ingredients needed in healing a partnership. Like a carefully balanced scale, humility must equal forgiveness or the imbalance will cause the relationship to topple. On one side of the scale is forgiveness—forgiveness the victim needs to extend toward the transgressor for the pain, heartache, darkness, betrayal and upheaval a transgressor has brought into a relationship. On the other side of the scale must be an equal portion of humility on the part of the transgressor—humility that includes a transgressor's willingness to overcome sinful tendencies and weaknesses, acknowledge the destruction and darkness brought in by sinful choices, and make gestures of restitution and reparation in the relationship.

If both of these are not present in equal proportion in the partnership, the relationship will not move forward but remain in constant imbalance. Contention, fighting, bickering, misunderstanding, resentment, anger, blame and bitterness are some of the fruits of this imbalance. Although the path of healing will never be easy, when both humility and forgiveness are present in equal proportion, increased understanding, revived trust, glimmers of hope, patience, renewed love, kindness and caring become manifest and grow stronger—"line upon line, precept upon precept." (D&C 98:12) The road becomes easier and less rocky; the darkness begins to lift and is replaced by growing light, peace and strength.

It should be strongly reasserted that finding this balance in the relationship will *never* occur at the outset or the beginning of the road to healing. It will only come through time, great effort, tears, frustration and pain as both partners try to work together to solve the tumultuous issues between them. If each person respectively turns to the Lord for strength and guidance in their separate lives, the Lord will then give the necessary ideas, feelings, insights and direction to move forward together. In other words, as each partner in the relationship becomes more whole by turning to the Savior, the healing and wholeness of the relationship becomes a natural by-product of their individual efforts.

It is true that healing in a broken relationship comes at great cost and only occurs through much toil, effort, tears and pain, but it *will* and *has* come to many who have sought the Savior and found this necessary balance of humility and forgiveness.

One woman reported this kind of healing in her marriage relationship after she and her husband incorporated these attributes into their lives after a crisis, a crisis which almost resulted in the breakup of their marriage. She said of this time, "I was ready to give up. I was ready to divorce (my husband). He seemed so hard-hearted and untouchable. I couldn't stand him anymore, and I didn't want to be with him and be subjected to all the pain he'd put me through throughout our marriage (because of his sexual addiction). I was done; it was over. I was through.

"We decided we would see our Bishop one more time before we actually divorced. During our discussion with him, the Bishop said he felt inspired to give us both blessings. In my blessing, the Lord told me that if I would turn to Him, He would make me conqueror of all things. I knew He meant that He could heal my marriage.

"After that night, my husband and I both decided to give our marriage another try. I need to say that the process that occurred afterward was truly amazing. It was miraculous. I am still in awe at the changes that occurred in (my husband). His heart seemed to soften. He became more patient than I was with the kids. He began treating me kindly, and I could tell he wanted to try and make our relationship better. His heart was in it this time; I could sense and see the changes in him. He wanted our marriage to work.

"As these changes occurred in him, I went through my own experiences. I remember the forgiveness that came into my heart and the healing that occurred within me. This healing was real and tangible. I awoke one morning some time after this and I felt at complete ease and rest—without any of the pain and burden I'd carried before (of the betrayal). I realized that I had truly forgiven him and that I felt healed inside—completely healed. This feeling was *real*.

"I promise you that healing can occur in a marriage. I have felt it. I testify that it can happen. It is as real as anything I've ever experienced. Anyone who is struggling in a relationship needs to hold on and trust the Lord. When He says He can heal, He can. I know it—because He healed me."

This example illustrates how the balance of forgiveness and humility ultimately led to the healing of a marriage. For many who struggle with broken marriages the road can be much longer, more tempestuous and full of extreme difficulties, but the principle still applies. When both partners seek for the attributes necessary to heal the relationship—that is, forgiveness on the part of the victim and humility on the part of the transgressor, the movement toward healing escalates dramatically. It should be remembered, however, that if this balance does not exist in equal proportion, healing of the relationship is thwarted. Roadblocks will only be removed as each of these attributes is adopted.

• *Victims Need as Much Healing as Transgressors*

It is essential to understand during the process of healing that spouses of transgressors need as much help and healing as transgressors themselves do. Mark H. Butler in his speech "Spiritual Exodus: Recovery From Addiction" said it this way: "The spouses of addicts have suffered in ways that you cannot know unless you speak with them. Spouses are as much in need of recovery and healing as their partners." (Ibid.)

Truly, as mentioned before, spouses of transgressors many times go through a grieving process as real and traumatic as death. One Bishop described a transgressor as having dealt with a "slow-growing cancer" in terms of his sexual addiction and the spouse of the transgressor suddenly "having lost a limb" when she found out about the addiction. That metaphor amply describes the trauma and devastation that a spouse suffers when discovering the truth about a partner's secret life. It can be emotionally crippling.

The shock, pain, anger and other emotions of the grieving process cannot be circumvented or glossed over; these emotions will come and go through varying degrees throughout the entire process of healing. Trying to skip, skim through or ignore these emotions only creates havoc in other areas of life. For instance, one woman said she tried to suppress her feelings regarding the pain surrounding her husband's sexual addiction so much so that her buried feelings bled over into other interactions with friends and associates. She would often become bitter, contentious and easily lose control of her anger in normal, every-day conversations. She acknowledged that it occurred because of displaced aggression—a fruit of her tempestuous marriage, not the behavior of others in her life. She had to learn to allow herself to grieve more fully and feel pain for the loss and uncertainty she felt in her relationship before she could move forward toward healing.

Getting through the pain and emotion caused by a spouse's sexual addiction is like walking through a treacherous valley; one can't just jump to the other side and be on top of the hill and through with the difficult journey. One must go step by step down one side of the tumultuous path and back up the other—a path adequately described in a hymn as "rugged and steep" with "briars and thorns" and "sharp stones" that "cut your feet as you struggle to rise." ("Does the Journey Seem Long," p. 127).

One woman described the devastating emotions of the grieving process she went through as she dealt with her broken marriage: "After I found out about my husband's (deep sexual addiction), for four to five months afterwards I was filled with the most excruciating pain. I spiritually ached inside—almost as if there was a vice around my heart squeezing it tighter and tighter. Sometimes it felt like it was literally squeezing life out of me. I didn't realize I had the capacity to hurt as much as I did.

"I spent many sleepless nights that felt as long as eternity. I could barely function and could only do the bare necessities to keep my family going. Sometimes I felt like I had stepped through a time warp and would one day wake up from this horrible dream I was having. It didn't seem like the pain and sorrow I was experiencing could be real.

"I hurt so much that there were times I would be driving and would have to pull over so I could sob. If I saw a movie or anything that reminded me of what I was experiencing, I would sob. If I looked at a family picture during the time I knew my husband was being untrue, I would sob. It hurt so much. I didn't know a person could produce as many tears as I have or hurt as deeply as I did.

"I remember the darkness and pain being so terrible that as I attended the temple one day, I wanted to plead with my Heavenly Father to take me home where I wouldn't keep hurting as I did—where my heart wouldn't hold all the agony it held. The only thing that kept me wanting to stay was my children. I knew I couldn't leave them yet and that they needed me. But that was the *only* thing I wanted to stay here for—the only thing.

"As more time passed, I still ached inside, but some of my intense pain started to lessen. I remember hearing once that the human brain has a tremendous capacity to forget pain, and I began to experience this. I'm grateful for it. I began to function better. Even though the pain had not disappeared—and would overcome me occasionally, it seemed to be more often like a dull ache than the overwhelming pain I could not handle previously.

"During this time, I noticed I started to become more angry at (my husband) instead of being as hurt and devastated. The anger felt better and easier to handle than the hurt I'd felt. I began to feel angry for my husband's choices—for the selfishness that had allowed him to do this to me and his children, for the deceit that he'd been involved in for such a long time, and for how he'd betrayed me and the children so terribly.

"I felt angry for the darkness he'd let into our lives, that he might have affected our children and caused them to sin, too. I felt angry and disillusioned that he'd treated our eternal covenants so lightly, that he had never truly cherished and loved me as a wife should be loved. I felt angry that he was willing to 'sell his birthright for a mess of pottage,' so to speak, and that he didn't seem to care or feel sorrow for the seriousness of his choices. It's almost like he didn't care about the eternal consequences of them.

"The contention increased a lot between us. I fought with (my husband) whenever I saw the behaviors I know must have either been a by-product of his addiction—things I put up with before because I didn't know where they came from, or behaviors that were caused by his addiction. I fought him whenever I felt controlled or manipulated, or whenever I felt he used anger or disapprobation to influence me or the children. It seemed like whenever we were together, we would end up fighting. We seldom had a good conversation. We had a few good times and memories, but they were very rare.

"Sometimes when we fought, my husband would leave me in anger and I would end up in turmoil, thinking our marriage would certainly end. I felt a dichotomy of feeling with the threat of his leaving. On one hand, I felt it might be easier for me to have him leave and then to start all over—to not have to deal with all the baggage and pain he'd put into our lives. On the other hand, his leaving would be difficult financially and on the kids and right now they were my first priority. Too, there were parts of me that didn't want to give up on the two of us working things out—despite how difficult it was.

"I remember after one heated argument between us, when I saw the anger and frustration my husband had for me, I had to face the cold reality of the realization, 'My husband could learn to hate me. He's losing his love for me.' It was devastating—to see so clearly that I could truly lose my husband's love and that in many ways, I already had. This, as hard as it was, became a turning point for me. I suddenly learned I could not change him or his feelings—and that I needed to be independent of him or I could be destroyed emotionally.

"I remember agonizing over our relationship one particular day. I worried about my husband's feelings and where our relationship was at, feeling as if I had no control over it at all. As I was thinking and feeling shaky and vulnerable, I heard the voice of the Lord whisper to me, 'Don't you trust him to me?' I knew the Lord was telling me that literally I had to let go of the reins with my husband. I had no control over him, and I had to turn him completely over to the Lord. I couldn't control the end product of what would happen to our marriage—or him.

"As I tried to incorporate this into my life—this process of literally turning my husband over to the Lord, I felt myself growing stronger. I was less affected by my husband's anger and disapprobation. I began to turn to the Lord for the feelings of completeness and wholeness that I needed whenever we had an argument or fight, or whenever I felt vulnerable in our relationship—which was often. I worried less about the future, trusting the Lord would take care of me—no matter what happened.

"As I became stronger with the Lord, it was interesting to see that our relationship began to grow stronger, too—little by little. It was partly the changes in me, but my husband began to change, too. He tried to be more patient with me and the children. He tried to see and understand how the consequences of his past choices affected me and he began to try and reach me in my hurting and pain. It's not that everything got rosy—it didn't. We still fought a great deal and had disagreements and misunderstandings. But our relationship did turn a corner. We began to feel a revival of some love and trust.

"I think what I've learned most from this difficult experience is that in the end, it only matters what the Lord thinks—not my husband or anyone else. It is only the Lord's approval that I need in my life, and if I have that, I can turn to Him in everything and then turn everything over to him—my life, my husband, my children, my marriage—everything. I can trust that the Lord will take care of me and grant unto me all the blessings His faithful children have if I, too, remain faithful.

"I've also learned that no matter what my husband did or didn't do—even if he expressed sorrow for his sins or if he tried to be kind to me, I couldn't get any healing from him or his behavior. I could only get the deep inward healing I needed from the Lord. I've finally come to understand what the scriptures mean when they say it is only through our Savior that we can find wholeness and happiness. This experience has taught me that everything good that I feel, that I experience or learn is from Him. He truly is the light and life of the world and the One we have to turn to for our own salvation.

"My husband and I still have many struggles—sometimes daily. Things can turn volatile in a moment. But I still hold onto a promise I received in a priesthood blessing that one day there will be healing and wholeness in my marriage and that I will have the deep relationship with my husband that I desire. This keeps me going through the rough patches.

"I don't know what to tell other women experiencing the pain I have—only that the Lord understands them and will help them, no matter where they are at. He loves them so much, and He aches for their pains and sorrows. He feels and understands every tear they shed. I have felt Him comfort me in my darkest hours when nothing or no one could reach me.

"I have learned much more deeply what the Savior's atonement means to me in my life—that it is a real redeeming process, not some ethereal idea that will be incorporated some time after we are dead. The power of the atonement is real; I feel the changes happening in my life right now in my heart as I become closer and closer to the Savior. I see the atonement working in my husband's life, too, as he is trying to cleanse it and become purified. I see the Savior teaching him things I could never teach him.

"I get teary when I think of the Savior and all He's done for me and for those who have to suffer like I've had to suffer. I love my Savior so much. I know without a doubt He will help anyone through the grief of a betrayal. In fact, that's the only way anyone will make it through. He suffered greatly so He could know how to do this for us, and I know He will—and does. I'll love Him eternally for that."

The reason the Lord places sexual sin second only to murder is because it is eternal law that where sexual sin has occurred, deep, devastating damage has been done to not only the transgressor but to innocent parties surrounding him. It must be remembered that only the Savior can heal the pain and wounds of this kind of betrayal. The pain and emotions that arise for the victims cannot be circumvented or quickly traversed. But the Savior will walk this rugged path of grieving step by step with these innocent victims who bear these great burdens, burdens that have come about through no fault of their own but through others' misuse of agency.

• *Individuals Need a Safe Environment—Outside of the Marriage Relationship—in Which to Express Feelings or Deal with Other Emotional Issues*

In all relationships we have seen that have moved toward healing and recovery after a pornography addiction, there has existed for each side of a partnership a safe environment in which each individual can express feelings and emotions, an environment independent of the other party. (Ideally the transgressor and a spouse will become this "safe environment" for each other as they move toward healing, but often there is too much devastation and destruction to find this kind of strength in a damaged relationship initially. For some, outside intervention is needed throughout the entire process of healing and rebuilding a relationship.)

These "safe environments" for each party may include talking with priesthood leaders, seeing marriage and family counselors, becoming a part of an addiction support group, finding a close friend who cares and understands, or seeking out family members or others with whom the person feels emotionally safe.

One woman stated that, "I would have never made it through my trials if I didn't have my friend to turn to that had gone through the exact same thing I was experiencing. She let me cry in her arms and shared my heartaches and sorrows. I know the Lord planted her in my life to help me through this, and I'll be eternally grateful for her influence. I would have never made it through this without her."

Another "safe environment" may include keeping a journal in which to report feelings, experiences, pains, insights, progression and setbacks. One woman said that, "In a little over four months I filled a complete journal with what I was experiencing (her marital problems after her husband's betrayal). My previous Journal took me over three years to fill."

• *Time*

Another essential ingredient needed on the long road to healing is time. This includes not only the necessary time set aside daily and weekly to try to work through problems and issues in a marriage, but a commitment to the great length of time that will be needed to heal a partnership after there has been a betrayal. As one marriage counselor said, "It is a willingness to stick with the process, realizing that it will take a long time for recovery, that is a key to recovery."

It is the willingness to work through difficult issues, solve contentious matters, struggle through arguments, try to recover from destructive fights, listen to what has caused injuries and pain and work through misunderstandings that will become the essential foundation for rebuilding. Once sin has been present in a relationship, the road to recovery will always be marked with difficulty and hardship; it is a natural by-product of sin. But the willingness to work through these difficulties and hardships is what will eventually bring the desired results of healing.

Because old ways of working through problems in a relationship are in many ways dysfunctional, new ways of relating must be established. As one marriage counselor once described it, "It's like moving out of the deep ruts on a road. It often feels uncomfortable when you try to get out, but once you do get out, the journey is much smoother." Oftentimes "rules" for this new kind of interaction must be established so couples can get out of the old "ruts" in their relationship.

One woman explained her experience this way: "Because we could hardly get through a discussion without a fight, our Bishop advised us to each take fifteen minutes—without interruption—to express ourselves and what we were feeling. There would be fifteen minutes of speaking for one person followed by fifteen minutes for the other. During that time, the other person could not say a word or the conversation would have to stop completely and not continue until the next day. This at least got us started talking without fighting all the time."

Oftentimes working through contentious issues needs to include third parties who can help establish rules that govern a couple's interaction. During the process of one couple working to heal their broken relationship, the wife said that she and her husband "had to see a counselor once a week. We each would make a list of the issues we could not work out together, and we would try to work on them with the counselor intervening. Sometimes we got so bad we had to call 'emergency sessions' with our counselor, but little by little we learned how to better handle our communication."

For another woman, she had to call "time outs" when she felt emotionally manipulated by her husband and chose to "withdraw" until she felt safe to move forward with him once more. She said, "I often felt controlled and manipulated by (my husband) during our discussions (in attempting to rebuild our relationship). I'd always succumbed to his anger and frustration before I knew about his addiction, so it seemed he always tried to resort to those behaviors whenever things got out of hand. Logically he could always beat me in an argument, too, so I felt I couldn't win when we fought. It would get so I would have to call a 'time out' and withdraw from speaking to him until I felt we could work through issues without what I saw as his trying to control and manipulate me as he had in the past. I was unwilling to accept the way he'd used to relate to me, and I would not give in until there was some compromise on his part."

Each couple progressing toward healing will have to establish new rules and boundaries in their relationships, similar to those stated in the examples above, in order to rebuild and heal. Though these "rules" will vary couple by couple, they will require time—not only time set aside to work through issues, but a commitment to the great length of time that will be needed to ultimately overcome difficulties in a damaged relationship.

Satan's Way vs. the Lord's Way

During the process of rebuilding, there will be a constant battle to handle circumstances either Satan's way or the Lord's way. Satan's paths will always cause worse and more extensive damage than what has already been caused; the Lord's way will encompass moves toward healing, wholeness and forgiveness. Learning the Lord's way will take time and effort and is not without tears and pain, but the Lord can and will work with and strengthen individuals trying to align their wills to His. As one woman said after her husband's deep betrayal, "I had to take a crash course in learning to become like the Savior." Through her efforts and the desire for repentance on the part of her husband, they were able to heal their deep wounds.

Remember:

Satan would have someone blame, manipulate and control a partner; the Lord would have someone try to love, forgive and help that person.

Satan would plant seeds of disgust, repulsion and bitterness for past mistakes and weaknesses; the Lord would cultivate compassion, forgiveness and sympathy.

Satan would continually bring past deeds forward, never letting them be forgotten; the Lord would ask that past misdeeds be given to Him, letting Him be the one who hands out judgment and retribution.

Satan would have someone hold relentlessly to hurts and injuries; the Lord invites that person to come to Him to have those wounds healed.

Satan would have someone judge harshly and with bitterness; the Lord would have someone leave judgment to Him.

Satan would make one feel as if overcoming the transgression is impossible, that weaknesses will always prevail; the Lord would have someone believe "I am able to make you holy" (D&C 60:7) and that He "knoweth the weakness of man and how to succor them who are tempted." (D&C 62:1)

Fruits that come from Satan's tactics include despair, feelings of hopelessness, depression, bitterness, anger, rage, contention, and retribution. Fruits that come from the Savior would include peace, inward calm, strength, comfort, wholeness, forgiveness, determination and hope.

Though it will always be a struggle between these two forces, more and more light and greater and greater peace will come into the lives of those who seek the Savior's way in the paths of healing. Satan would only create greater wounds, deeper darkness and lasting misery. It is only the Savior's hand that can rebuild broken relationships and bring happiness back into a marriage.

As Jeffrey R. Holland once said:

> Every one of us has times when we need to know things will get better. . . .For emotional and spiritual stamina, everyone needs to be able to look forward to some respite, to something pleasant and renewing and hopeful, whether that blessing be near at hand or still some distance ahead.
>
> . . .My declaration is that this is what the gospel of Jesus Christ offers us, especially in times of need. There *is* help. There *is* happiness. There really *is* light at the end of the tunnel. It is the Light of the World, the Bright and Morning Star, the "light that is endless, that can never be darkened." (Mosiah16:19) It is the very Son of God Himself. . . .It is the return of hope, and Jesus is the Sun. To any who may be struggling to see that light and find that hope, I say: Hold on. Keep trying. God loves you. Things will improve. Christ comes to you in His "more excellent ministry" with a future of "better promises." (Hebrews 8:6)
>
> . . .I think of those who suffer from sin— their own or someone else's—who need to know there is a way back and that happiness can be restored. . . .To all of these. . .I say: Cling to your

faith. Hold on to your hope.

. . .Even if you cannot always see that silver lining on the clouds, God can, for He is the very source of the light you seek. He does love you, and He knows your fears. He hears your prayers, He is your Heavenly Father, and surely He matches with His own the tears His children shed.

. . .Christ knows better than all others that the trial of life can be very deep and we are not shallow people if we struggle with them.

. . .*He knows that for the faithful things will be made right soon enough. He is a King; He speaks for the crown; He knows what can be promised.* (*Ensign,* Nov. 1999, pp. 36-37)

Truly, promised blessings will come to those who seek the Lord for healing and strength in their damaged relationships. As one woman was told in a priesthood blessing, the Lord would give her spiritual manna sufficient to see her through the trials of each day. He also promised that, as the frost on a winter's morning is slowly melted by the sun, so, too, healing in her heart and marriage would come. He cautioned that this process would be slow but promised that it would happen—to the point where all she experienced would one day only be a "dark memory."

And now, verily I say unto you, and what I say unto one I say unto all, be of good cheer, little children; for I am in your midst, and I have not forsaken you;

And inasmuch as you have humbled yourselves before me, the blessings of the kingdom are yours. (D&C 61:36-37)

Truly, the blessings of the kingdom are a gift to all willing to turn to the Savior through their trials and sufferings as they try to move toward wholeness and healing in relationships that have been damaged by pornography addiction.

9
Light Amidst the Storm

Light for the Transgressor

Transgressors working to overcome sins can come to taste of the pure, tender love the Savior has for His lost sheep. Through continued efforts toward repentance, our Savior's light will enter their broken lives in greater abundance. They will begin to sense His deep, yearning desire to apply the saving power of His atonement in their lives. He has said in Mark 2:17: "They that are whole have no need of the physician, but they that are sick: I came not to call the righteous but sinners to repentance."

The Lord's love and mercy for a transgressor is so beautifully illustrated in the Lord's parables of the lost sheep, the lost coin and of the prodigal son. The Lord truly does leave the "ninety and nine" to "go after that which is lost." (Luke 15:4) "Joy shall be in heaven," He tells us, "over one sinner that repenteth, more than over ninety and nine just persons, which need no repentance." (Luke 15:7) His is a pure and holy rejoicing over one who "was dead, and is alive again; [one who]

was lost, and is found." (Luke 15:24)

A transgressor must come to trust that mercy and forgiveness are waiting for him as gifts from our Savior. As the Prophet Joseph Smith said, "There is never a time when the spirit is too old to approach God. All are within the reach of pardoning mercy, who have not committed the unpardonable sin." (*Teachings*, p. 191) The scriptures state, "Even now, if he will hearken unto my voice, it shall be well with him." (D&C 124:110)

A Mighty Change of Heart

Transgressors can come to feel the miraculous power of the Lord's inward cleansing and the "mighty change" of heart that goes along with it, in that they "have no more disposition to do evil, but to do good continually." (Mosiah 5:2) Through this, transgressors will come to taste of the Lord's everlasting patience with them in working out their salvation.

This concept can be illustrated by the struggles of a woman who watched a man battle in-depthly his problems and challenges. One day as she described his challenges to a friend, she said, "He was doing so good at first. He was staying strong and faithful. But it's like the story of Peter. He began walking on the water, but when the wind and the waves came, he fell."

Right after she'd said this, a powerful impression came from the Lord into her mind. The Lord said, "But *immediately* I extended my hand."

> And in the fourth watch of the night Jesus went unto them, walking on the sea.
> And when the disciples saw him walking on the sea, they were troubled, saying, It is a spirit; and they cried out for fear.
> But straightway Jesus spake unto them, saying, Be of good cheer; it is I; be not afraid.
> And Peter answered him and said, Lord if it be thou, bid me come unto thee on the water.

> And he said, Come. And when Peter was
> come down out of the ship, he walked on the water,
> to go to Jesus.
>
> But when he saw the wind boisterous, he
> was afraid; and beginning to sink, he cried, saying,
> Lord, save me.
>
> *And immediately Jesus stretched forth his hand,
> and caught him.* (Matthew 14:25-31, italics added)

This woman came to learn that the Savior would immediately extend a hand to someone sinking because of weaknesses or lack of faith. In His love, He will reach out to those thus struggling in patience, mercy and understanding. "In all their afflictions he was afflicted," the scriptures tell us. "And the angel of his presence saved them; and in his love, and in his pity, he redeemed them, and bore them, and carried them." (D&C 133:53)

One man, who had fallen and participated in pornography during attempts to cleanse his life, once felt overwhelming love and mercy from the Lord *directly after* one time of participation. He became awed at the evidence of the Lord's mercy for him even after he had sinned, and this experience became an anchor to him in his efforts toward future healing.

A similar experience has been described by Steven A. Cramer in *The Worth of a Soul*. He told of an experience he had after a life-long addiction to pornography followed by an affair. During the first few days after his affair, he struggled with the intense desire to go to the other woman and continue their adulterous relationship. He said:

> I was supposed to be doing income taxes,
> but I ignored my last appointment and parked by
> a canal bank where I could walk alone. I wanted
> desperately to pray for help, but I was too ashamed
> to pray. I had not prayed for so long, and now,
> after my sin, how could I dare to approach God for

help?

I continued walking and fearing and sobbing until I finally could stand it no longer. I burst forth with an expression of sorrow for what I had done. I explained how I had messed up everybody's life and that I just didn't know how I could withstand the temptation of going back to that girl. I just had to have help resisting, or I would slip back to her in spite of my resolves.

The moment I finished my tormented plea for help—that very instant—the Lord's answer was there. Instantly His voice was in my mind, soothing me and reassuring me that I was not alone. His peace encompassed me and soothed my fears, witnessing to me that I was still loved. Loved? Yes! Loved no less than before I had committed this terrible act. The message was as clear and unmistakable as if He had appeared before my eyes in the flesh. There was absolutely no doubt that He had heard my prayer. Again I wept, overwhelmed by His response. (p.33)

Because of this experience, Steven Cramer then had the inward fortitude to go home to his wife, confess, and begin the necessary steps toward healing their broken relationship.

Becoming Cleansed

As with Alma, a soul once "racked with torment" and "harrowed up by the memory of. . .many sins" (Alma 36:12) can taste of the Savior's atoning and cleansing power. When Alma thought on our Savior, he tells us:

I cried within my heart: O Jesus, thou Son of God, have mercy on me, who am in the gall of bitterness, and am encircled about by the everlasting chains of death.

And now, behold, when I thought this, I could remember my pains no more; yea, I was harrowed up by the memory of my sins no more.

> And oh, what joy, and what marvelous light
> I did behold; yea, my soul was filled with joy as
> exceeding as was my pain! (Alma 36:18-20)

Though this process for transgressors might not be as immediate as Alma's, it can be as life changing and far-reaching as his experience became. This can happen to any transgressor willing to look to the "light and life of the world; yea, a light that is endless, that can never be darkened." (Mosiah 16:9)

Sometimes it's as simple as solely "looking" to the Savior in thought and prayer. "O, my brethren," Alma stated,

> if ye could be healed my merely casting about your
> eyes that ye might be healed, would ye not behold
> quickly, or would ye rather harden your hearts in
> unbelief, and be slothful, that ye would not cast
> about your eyes, that ye might perish?
> . . .If not so, then cast about your eyes and
> begin to believe in the Son of God, that he will come
> to redeem his people, and that he shall suffer and
> die to atone for their sins.
> . . .I desire that ye shall plant this word in
> your hearts. (Alma 33:21-23)

"In the Day of my Wisdom" (Helaman 15:16)

The Lord has told us in the scriptures, "In the day of my wisdom they shall return again unto me." (Helaman 15:16) Though He is speaking about a people in this instance, this scripture can also be applied to transgressors. In working with transgressors, the Lord, in His mercy, will most often bring to light sins and transgressions when there is the greatest possibility of healing. It may not seem the Lord has a hand in engineering events like this, but as He has said, He "knoweth all things from the beginning, wherefore, he prepareth a way to accomplish all his works among the children of men." (1 Nephi 9:6)

These times of darkness and trial will one day be

turned into blessings. As Terry C. Warner said, "Heaven, once obtained, will work backward and turn even. . .agony into glory." (Warner, BYU Women's Conference, 2000, "Why we Forgive") The scriptures say it this way: "Let your hearts be comforted; for all things shall work together for good to them that walk uprightly, and to the sanctification of the church." (D&C 100:15)

Transgressors can rest assured that although the Lord has "suffered. . .affliction(s) to come upon them, wherewith they have been afflicted, in consequence of their transgressions" that He "will own them, and they shall be mine in that day when I come to make up my jewels." (D&C 101:2-3)

> Ye were the servants of sin, but ye have obeyed from the heart that form of doctrine which was delivered you.
>
> Being then made free from sin, ye became the servants of righteousness.
>
> I speak after the manner of men because of the infirmity of your flesh: for as ye have yielded your members servants to uncleanness and to iniquity unto iniquity, even so now yield your members servants to righteousness unto holiness.
>
> For when ye were servants of sin, ye were free from righteousness.
>
> What fruit had ye then in those things whereof ye are now ashamed? For the end of those things is death.
>
> But now, being made free from sin, and become servants to God, ye have your fruit unto holiness, and to the end everlasting life.
>
> For the wages of sin is death; but the gift of God is eternal life through Jesus Christ our Lord. (Romans 6:17-23)

Light for the Those Working with Transgressors

Those willing to work with transgressors in overcoming

their sins can find comfort and strength from a special promise given by the Lord: "If it so be that you should labor all your days in crying repentance unto this people, and bring, save it be one soul unto me," He tells us, "how great shall be your joy with him in the kingdom of my Father!" (D&C 18:15) Notice the Lord puts an exclamation point at the end of the verse. This indicates the depth and magnitude of His promise.

Mark H. Butler in his speech "Spiritual Exodus: Recovery from Addiction" said it this way: "If there is one beautiful flower that can bloom among the thorns of addiction, it is the nobility manifest in covenant relationships as one soul—in pure, Christlike love—consecrates his or her heart, might, mind and strength to saving another. They are literally saviors on mount Zion." (*BYU Families Under Fire Conference*, Oct. 3, 2002)

Many of these souls who do this come to see and realize that these transgressors have often come on foreordained missions by the Lord to cleanse lineages that have been plagued by sexual or other grievous sins. Like the Lamanites,

> it is because of the traditions of their fathers that caused them to remain in their state of ignorance; therefore the Lord will be merciful unto them and prolong their existence in the land.
>
> And at some period of time they will be brought to believe in his word, and to know of the incorrectness of the traditions of their fathers; and many of them will be saved, for the Lord will be merciful unto all who call on his name. (Alma 9: 16, 17)

Just as the Lord will many times assign a valiant woman to work with a transgressor, so has He often assigned valiant spirits these missions of cleansing. He has trusted in the fact that these great souls would strive beyond the wickedness and damaging influence of intergenerational traits or other weaknesses to overcome them and finally begin a pure and

chosen generation. He promises, "He that is weak among
you shall hereafter be made strong." (D&C 50:16) The Lord
truly loves His wandering souls with a depth and breadth one
only begins to sense when working hand in hand with Him in
healing the life of a transgressor. "If any man among you be
strong in spirit, let him take with him him that is weak," He
tells us, "that he may be edified in all meekness, that he may
become strong also." (D&C 84:106).

The Lord will *never* forget the efforts of His servants in
working with these transgressors. He promises:

> For God is not unrighteous to forget your
> work and labour of love, which ye have shewed
> toward his name, in that ye have ministered to the
> saints, and do minister.
>
> And we desire that every one of you do
> shew the same diligence to the full assurance of
> hope unto the end:
>
> That ye be not slothful, but followers of
> them who through faith and patience inherit the
> promises.
>
> For when God made promise to Abraham,
> because he could swear by no greater, he sware by
> himself,
>
> Saying, Surely blessing I will bless thee, and
> multiplying I will multiply thee.
>
> And so, after he had patiently endured, he
> obtained the promise.
>
> . . .Which *hope* we have as an anchor of the
> soul. (Hebrews 6:10-15, 19)

Compensating Blessings

Those who have taken upon themselves the burdens of
working with transgressors need to understand that one day
the Lord will compensate them. He will make up for every
unjust burden placed upon their shoulders because of having
to bear the unrighteous choices of others. Blessings will come

abundantly to them to help them through times of trial and challenge, as well. The Lord will "impart unto [them] of [His] Spirit, which shall enlighten [their] minds, which shall fill [their] souls with joy" (D&C 11:13). He will grant compensatory blessings from heaven and give "strength such as is not known to men" (D&C 24:12) to those attempting to do this work. He will also help them bear "with patience the persecution which [is] heaped upon them" (Alma 1:25) because of transgressors' initial inability to accept blame for their own behaviors.

The Lord will also give blessings of peace to those working with transgressors during times of oppressive darkness when they cannot overcome trials, challenges and turmoil on their own. Like the Lamanites who were converted by Nephi and Lehi's great faith, the "cloud of darkness" will be "removed from overshadowing" them when they call upon the Lord in faith. "Peace, peace be unto you because of your faith in my Well Beloved, who was from the foundation of the world," the scriptures tell us. (Helaman 5:41, 47) The Lord promises: "The work of righteousness shall be peace; and the effect of righteousness quietness and assurance for ever." (Isaiah 32:17)

"The Prayers of the Faithful Shall be Heard" (2 Nephi 26:15)

Those working with transgressors should be reminded that their prayers of faith can be a compelling, life-changing force in the lives of those who are trying to become clean. "For if there be no faith among the children of men God can do no miracle among them," Ether 12:12 tells us.

> . . .It was the faith of Nephi and Lehi *that wrought the change* upon the Lamanites.
>
> . . .It was the faith of Ammon and his brethren *that wrought so great a miracle* among the Lamanites.
>
> . . .And neither at any time hath any wrought miracles until after their faith; wherefore they first believed in the Son of God. (Ether 12:14-

15, 18, italics added)

"And Christ hath said: If ye will have faith in me ye shall have power to do whatsoever thing is expedient in me," we have been promised. (Moroni 7:33)

It was the faith of Mosiah that saved his son, Ammon, when he had "sunk to the earth" (Alma 19:14) and had become helpless. When an angry man

> drew his sword and went forth that he might let it fall upon Ammon to slay him. . .behold, he fell dead.
>
> Now we see that Ammon could not be slain, for the Lord had said unto Mosiah, his father: I will spare him, and *it shall be unto him according to thy faith*—therefore, Mosiah trusted him unto the Lord. (Alma 19:22-23, italics added)

It is truly by faith that "all things are fulfilled"—

> Wherefore, whoso believeth in God might with surety hope for a better world, yea, even a place at the right hand of God, which hope cometh of faith, maketh an anchor to the souls of men, which would make them sure and steadfast, always abounding in good works, being led to glorify God." (Ether 12:3- 4)

Maintaining Light during Times of Darkness and Struggle

The Lord has promised, "When thou passeth through the waters, I will be with thee; and through the rivers, they shall not overflow thee: when thou walkest through the fire, thou shalt not be burned; neither shall the flame kindle upon thee. Fear not, I am with thee." (Isaiah 43:2,5)

President Ezra Taft Benson, in his article "Do Not Despair," (*Ensign*, Nov. 1974) gave some powerful insights regarding how to maintain this kind of hope and strength through troubled times. He said, "To help us from being overcome by the devil's designs of despair, discouragement, depression, and despondency, the Lord has provided at least a dozen ways which, if followed, will lift our spirits and send us on our way rejoicing." He then lists these important ways as follows:

Repentance. "Sin pulls a man down into despondency and despair. . . .A man would do well to examine himself to see that he is in harmony with all of God's laws," he tells us.

As President Benson has counseled, we need to pray, whether we are transgressors or the victims of transgression, that all of our sins will be overcome and forgiven so that we can "strip ourselves of all uncleanness." (Mormon 9:28) As it says in Psalm 51:

> Have mercy on me, O God, according to thy lovingkindness: according unto the multitude of thy tender mercies blot out my transgressions.
> Wash me thoroughly from mine iniquity, and cleanse me from my sin.
> For I acknowledge my transgressions.
> . . .Purge me. . .and I shall be clean: wash me, and I shall be whiter than snow.
> Hide thy face from my sins, and blot out my iniquities.
> Create in me a clean heart, O God; and renew a right spirit within me. (1-3; 7; 9-10)

With this kind of repentance, the Lord gives us a powerful promise. "For I will be merciful to their unrighteousness," He tells us, "and their sins and their iniquities will I remember no more." (Hebrews 8:12)

Prayer. "Prayer can put us in touch with God," President Benson continues, "our greatest source of comfort and counsel."

This second step President Benson has suggested is truly the "boon to mortals giv'n" that will "unite (our) soul(s) with heaven." (*Hymns*, p. 144) Prayers during times of trial and struggle are often answered immediately and powerfully. This act of prayer can become an effective tool in finding peace amidst the storms that arise because of sin.

For example, one woman prayed during a time of darkness and struggle to know of the Lord's awareness of her in an intimate and personal way. She felt lost and forsaken and needed to somehow feel His reassuring love through her trials. As she attended a choir concert for one of her young sons, the words to the song "Candle on the Water" hit her deeply—as if the Lord was speaking the words to her. Not certain that this was her answer, however, she prayed to know if this was His "sign" of His loving awareness and if it was, how could she know?

As she got in her car a short time after the concert to run an errand, the moment she turned on the radio the song came on once again, leaving her in unrestrained tears. She had received a beautiful confirmation of her prayers and the Lord's reassuring voice through the words:

> *I'll be your candle on the water,*
> *My love for you will always burn.*
> *I know you're lost and drifting,*
> *But the clouds are lifting.*
> *Don't give up you have Somewhere to turn.*

> *I'll be your candle on the water,*
> *`Til every wave is warm and bright.*
> *My Soul is there beside you,*
> *Let this candle guide you.*
> *Soon you'll see a golden stream of light.*

> *A cold and friendless tide has found you,*
> *Don't let this stormy darkness pull you down.*
> *I'll paint a ray of hope around you,*
> *Circling in the air.*
> *Lighted by a prayer.*

I'll be your candle on the water,
This flame inside of me will grow.
Keep holding on, you'll make it.
Here's my Hand so take it.
Look for Me reaching out to show,
As sure as rivers flow,
I'll never let you go.
I'll never let you go.
I'll never let you go. (Kasha, Wonderland Music
Company, 1976; capitalization added)

This became a treasured memory for her and she found strength from the words often. Prayer can bring this kind of solace and direction to those seeking for it through times of darkness and challenge.

Service. "'When you find yourselves a little gloomy,' said President Lorenzo Snow, 'look around you and find somebody that is in a worse plight than yourself; go to him and find out what the trouble is, then try to remove it with the wisdom which the Lord bestows upon you; and the first thing you know, your gloom is gone, you feel light, the spirit of the Lord is upon you, and everything seems illuminated.' (*Conference Report*, 6 Apr. 1899, pp. 2-3)"

This lesson quoted by President Benson is not only applicable to victims of transgression, but can also apply to transgressors—who in sharing their experiences of overcoming sin can be instruments of healing others suffering in the same way. Alma is a wonderful example of someone rendering this type of service. He never delineated his sins, but he spoke often of how he overcame darkness in his life. Even though Alma himself had participated in grievous sin, this did not stop him from boldly warning his son Corianton about Corianton's sexual sins. He said to his son,

I would to God that ye had not been guilty
of so great a crime. I would not dwell upon your

crimes, to harrow up your soul, if it were not for
your own good.

But behold, ye cannot hide your crimes
from God; and except ye repent they will stand as a
testimony against you at the last day.

Now my son, I would that ye should repent
and forsake your sins, and go no more after the lusts
of your eyes, but cross yourself in all these things;
for except ye do this ye can in nowise inherit the
kingdom of God. Oh, remember, and take it upon
you, and cross yourself in these things. (Alma 39:
7-9)

Alma's words and counsel became a powerful impetus that
helped his son overcome his transgressions.

Steven A. Cramer, who has written such meaningful
works as *The Worth of a Soul, Great Shall be Your Joy, Putting on
the Armor of God* and other similar books is another example
of this kind of service. He is someone who has used his
experiences of past sin to bring strength and healing to many
struggling to overcome darkness in their own lives. He has
adopted the teaching in Psalm 51:12-13: "Restore me unto
the joy of thy salvation. . . .*Then* will I teach transgressors thy
ways; and sinners shall be converted unto thee." Transgressors
who willingly do this will find their own healing taking place
in greater measure. As they "teach. . .an everlasting hatred
against sin and iniquity" and teach others to "withstand every
temptation of the devil, with their faith on the Lord Jesus
Christ," (Alma 37:32-33) they will find growth and meaning
from their experiences, even painful ones.

Also, those who have been hurt by transgressors can
find healing and strength in serving others. One woman, who
had been betrayed deeply by her husband, shared an experience
that illustrates how service blessed her. She said, "It seemed all
I did was think of myself and my trials. I always seemed to
be talking about myself and what I was going through. One

morning I pleaded, 'Please, Heavenly Father. Please let me find and help someone else today instead of only thinking about me.'"

She continued, "A short time later, I ran into a woman and could tell immediately from her eyes that she was struggling. I took her into my car and let her talk and share all that she was experiencing. Afterward, I couldn't believe how light and happy I felt. My own troubles seemed to lessen and I was grateful to be an instrument in the Lord's hands in helping someone else."

Work. "We should work at taking care of the spiritual, mental, social, and physical needs of ourselves and those whom we are charged to help," President Benson also reminds us.

Hard work in the crucial areas President Benson has pointed out will help in two important ways. It will help keep transgressors occupied in righteous endeavors and less inclined to fall into patterns of previous behavior that led to sin. Work may also help an injured party overcome wounds without the lingering tendency to dwell unnecessarily on past hurts and pains, which can and will canker a soul with bitterness, anguish, despair and darkness. Though it's not always easy to extend this kind of effort through times of challenge and difficulty, physical and emotional strength will increase incrementally with continued efforts in these areas.

Health. "The condition of our physical bodies can affect our spirits," President Benson counseled.

As President Benson points out, our physical state can influence how we feel spiritually, mentally and emotionally. Our physical condition must be especially safeguarded during times of intense emotional pain and trauma, when we are much more susceptible to stress and stress-related illnesses. Getting the necessary sleep, water, exercise, rest and proper food is essential or our bodies get too run down and drained to deal adequately with ongoing trials. Sometimes medical help needs to be sought in keeping this balance. Health should be carefully nurtured and maintained as much as possible.

Reading—scriptures and modern revelation. "Many a man in his hour of trial has turned to the *Book of Mormon* and been enlightened, enlivened, and comforted," President Benson said. "The Psalms in the Old Testament have a special food for the soul of one in distress."

As President Benson has claimed, the Psalms can truly become a balm for those struggling with intense trials. The following Psalms are just a few examples that show this:

> The Lord will give strength unto his people; the Lord will bless his people with peace. (29:11)

> *The righteous cry*, and the Lord heareth, and delivereth them out of all their troubles.
> The Lord is nigh unto them that are of a broken heart; and saveth such as be of a contrite spirit.
> Many *are* the afflictions of the righteous: but the Lord delivereth him out of them all. (34:17-19)

> God is our refuge and our strength, a very present help in trouble.
> Therefore we will not fear. . .
> Be still and know that I *am* God. (46:1-2, 10)

> In the shadow of thy wings will I make my refuge, until these calamities be overpast. (57:1)

> Forsake me not when my strength faileth. (71:9)

> Then they cry unto the Lord in their trouble, and he bringeth them out of their distresses.
> He maketh the storm a calm, so that the waves thereof are still.
> Then they are glad because they be quiet; so he bringeth them to their desired haven. (107: 28-30)

Through God we shall do valiantly. (108:
13)

They that sow in tears shall reap in joy.
(126:5)

Insights such as these are soothing to a soul looking for comfort and strength through the scriptures. The Psalms, other scriptures and modern-day revelation can be a powerful source of this comfort in times of distress and trial.

Blessings. One can "seek for a blessing under the hands of the priesthood" for "solace and direction," President Benson advised.

As President Benson has reminded us, many transgressors and those working with them can receive priesthood blessings which can be one of the most meaningful and powerful sources of comfort, strength and direction. For example, one woman, in the initial stages of pain and shock in finding out about the sins of her husband, was told that if she continued to be faithful during this difficult trial, everything would be "restored unto her four-fold" and that these afflictions would "be but a small moment." Anchors and promises like these are available to everyone going through similar situations.

Priesthood blessings can also be a powerful buffer against the powers of the evil spirits that are trying to threaten the sanctity of a home and family. One woman had been promised through a blessing that those evil spirits would be cast out and that "guardian angels would stand arm in arm outside her home" to protect them from the influences that had plagued her family. Priesthood blessings can bring this promised heavenly protection to those who seek it.

Transgressors can garner great strength through priesthood blessings, as well. Through these the Lord can counsel, direct and show His genuine love and caring. One transgressor was told that he would be "blessed to overcome temptation" and that his "confidence would wax strong in the presence of the Lord." He was also "blessed to know of Heavenly Father's unconditional love" for him. This gave him light and comfort during a difficult time of trial and temptation as he was striving to overcome his sins.

Fasting. "A certain kind of devil goes not out except by fasting and prayer, the scripture tells us. (See Mark 9:29) Periodic fasting can help clear up the mind and strengthen the body and the spirit," President Benson said.

As President Benson has stated, fasting truly can be the tool that gives us emotional and spiritual strength, unlocking the door to needed answers when one's own strength and insights become depleted. Once one learns to effectively tap into this incredible power, fasting often becomes one of the first avenues used in seeking the Lord's help and guidance.

The story in Mark 9 in the *New Testament* powerfully illustrates this concept. One woman felt led to this story as she watched her brother struggle through horrific trials and challenges. Though she wanted to help him, she didn't feel as if she could offer direct support and she agonized over how she might assist him in overcoming his difficulties. Great insights came to her as she read the story about a man who had brought his struggling, tormented son to Jesus to be healed—after the disciples could do nothing to help him. Through the father's faith, Jesus

> rebuked the foul spirit, saying unto him, *Thou* dumb and deaf spirit, I charge thee, come out of him, and enter no more into him.
>
> And *the spirit* cried, and rent [the boy] sore, and came out of him.
>
> . . .Jesus took [the boy] by the hand, and lifted him up; and he arose. (Mark 9:25-27)

The disciples later came to Jesus and asked, "Why could we not cast him out?" (Mark 9:28)

Jesus answered, "This kind can come forth by nothing, but by prayer and fasting." (Mark 9:29)

When this woman read this story, she knew the only way she could help her brother was by consistent, regular fasting. She felt intuitively fasting would be the only thing—the sole key—that would help him overcome those things that tormented him. Through subsequent times of intense prayer and fasting, she began to see the fruits of her spiritual efforts in her brother's life. Little by little strength and enlightenment came to him, ultimately producing what she would term complete healing and wholeness. She believed these were the direct results of the impression to fast and pray for him.

Friends. "The fellowship of true friends who can hear you out, share your joys, help carry your burdens, and correctly counsel you is priceless," President Benson continued.

President Benson's words ring true especially for those dealing with the challenges that come from addiction. As mentioned previously, a trusted confidante for both a transgressor and those who have been affected by his choices becomes a key element in the healing process. Friends willing to talk, counsel with and listen to those struggling with sin or the consequences of them become invaluable, treasured resources to others desperately needing this kind of intervention. One woman spoke of a sister who had been a great strength and friend to her during her divorce, which came after a prolonged pornography addiction of her husband. Her sister's love, counsel and guidance became the only source of refuge and comfort she had.

Ideally, a transgressor and his wife can also become close confidantes during the process of healing. Though this will not happen initially, as a couple progresses toward healing, it can occur. One woman was told in a priesthood blessing to "walk beside" her husband who had transgressed, "not in front of him or behind him." Through this counsel, she learned to share her husband's struggles and walk the path with him, especially when he encountered temptation. He learned to turn to her during times of difficulty instead of fighting the battle alone. He told her once, "I felt I've had to fight the enemy with only a machine gun. Now that I have you to help me, I am fighting the enemy with a tank." They literally became closer friends during the healing process in spite of the areas in their lives that still needed revamping.

Her husband, too, learned to become a source of strength and healing for her in her struggles—and helped her begin to overcome the deep wounds she'd sustained because of his sins. He became more helpful, caring, concerned and conscientious of her continuing need to be nourished, strengthened and comforted.

Music. "Inspiring music may fill the soul with heavenly thoughts, move one to righteous actions, or speak peace to the soul," President Benson said.

Along with what President Benson has suggested, music, especially hymns, can comfort and cleanse souls—in a similar way that priesthood blessings can. Many times listening to hymns will bring healing when other sources of strength seem distant or unobtainable. One woman going through her trials said she "listened to the hymns almost constantly" through the intensity of her difficulties. This helped bring needed calm, peace and spiritual protection. There were other times when certain lines of hymns would come into her mind, bringing her much-needed direction, peace or comfort during her hardships.

Endurance. "There are times when you simply have to righteously hang on and outlast the devil until his depressive spirit leaves you," President Benson said.

This statement of President Benson becomes especially true for a transgressor who has become subjected to the buffetings of the adversary in his life. When Satan is persistent and unrelenting in his attacks, a transgressor must hold on knowing that because of his desires for righteousness and healing, soon the Lord's light will push away the darkness that has come as a consequence of unrighteous actions. Often it truly is "outlasting the devil," not letting the devil's venom, darkness and oppression become an integral part of life.

Those who are injured many times have to "righteously hang on and outlast the devil," as well. Sometimes darkness and trials seem too great to bear, especially when brought in by the effects of others' choices. Enduring faith and prayer can become keys to helping overcome these tribulations. George A. Smith quoted his cousin, the Prophet Joseph Smith, when he said, "He (the Prophet) told me that I should never get discouraged, whatever difficulties might surround me. If I were sunk into the lowest pit in Nova Scotia and all the Rocky Mountains piled on top of me, I ought not to be discouraged, but hang on, exercise faith, and keep up good courage, and I should come out on the top of the heap." (Jarvis, *George A. Smith Family*, p. 54)

As Psalm 69 says, "Let not the waterflood overflow me, neither let the deep swallow me up, and let not the pit shut her mouth upon me. Hear me, O Lord; for thy lovingkindness is good: turn unto me according to the multitude of thy tender mercies. (15-16)

Goals. "A man who is pressing forward to accomplish worthy goals can put despondency under his feet," President Benson concluded. (*Ensign*, 1974, p. 65)

This last step by President Benson can be applied to all aspects of life and not solely to everyday routines. Sometimes increasing time with hobbies or other outside interests can be powerfully beneficial in overcoming the darkness caused by intense trials. One woman found that some of the goals and aspirations she had put aside during her earlier years became sources of inspiration and happiness when she adopted them once again into her life. This helped her find joy amidst her continuing burdens.

Other keys to maintaining light during darkness. There are a few other key factors to maintaining light amidst storms of trials and adversity, besides those of President Benson above, that should be mentioned. These keys include: temple attendance and attendance at church meetings; being in nature as much as possible; and surrounding oneself with the light and love that come from childrens' pure spirits. Those struggling, too, should pray often to have ministering angels and those beyond the veil help and attend them in their efforts to protect and heal a home and family subjected to darkness because of someone's unrighteous choices.

Temple Attendance. Though temple attendance is not always an option for transgressors who have faced church action, others who attend may yearn to feel the strength and peace that comes from this sacred place. The temple can become a haven where dark forces cannot abide. Comfort, healing and inspiration come in abundance, and the spirit of this sacred place can enter into a home of one who has worthily participated. This spirit will then become an added protection against evil forces whose only intent is to harm or destroy.

Transgressors who cannot actually go inside the temple doors may many times find peace on the temple grounds. Going nearby a temple can become an instrument of healing and peace during times of emotional turmoil.

Attendance at church meetings. Attending meetings is so important for those struggling through times of darkness, especially for a transgressor who has faced church action. Even though this can be a difficult step, the Lord has ordained these times of instruction and worship to bring needed strength, direction and peace to His children.

Mark H. Butler in his speech "Spiritual Exodus: Recovery From Addiction" included attending church and other positive activities as powerful steps toward recovery. He said:

> I encourage clients to cleave to every positive, protective influence and activity they qualify for. They must not let feelings of unworthiness keep them from church, from praying, from seeking strength in the scriptures, from serving and cherishing their spouse, from the laughter and love of their children. They

must access every single positive influence they can qualify for and hold onto those with tenacious, pit-bull determination. Building from the positive is a great resource for recovery. *(BYU Families Under Fire Conference, Oct. 3, 2002)*

Enjoying nature. Many times nature can be a place to escape the buffetings of dark spirits that like to surround a transgressor's home and family. One woman, before knowing she had been battling evil influences from the choices of her husband, often found herself longing to go outside—the only place she would feel at peace. Nature can soothe and calm the soul and help keep one better in touch with the Creator of all things.

Children. Children's unconditional love and pure spirits can often bring solace and consolation to a struggling soul. Surrounding oneself with this influence is often a tremendous comfort and source of peace. One mother spoke of a time when she held her baby close to her heart for lengthy periods, finding from him needed peace as she was facing times of heartache and struggle in her home.

Prayers for protection. Appealing to the Lord for protection by His holy angels and those who have passed beyond the veil can be powerful in terms of comfort and strength during the process of healing. One woman literally felt the attendant strength from grandparents who had passed on as she walked through difficult trials brought on by the sins of her husband. Another woman felt the presence and peace brought by a brother who had passed on early in his life and she could testify of the concern and caring he held for her and her family. She had special sacred experiences that let her know he was watching over her and those she loved.

All of the above keys can be powerful, effective instruments in bringing greater light and comfort amidst times of trial and heartache. By adopting these beneficial principles, those struggling can more readily avoid the darkness, pain and

hurt that Satan continually tries to bring in and thus allow the
light of the Savior more fully into their lives. As the Savior
promises,

> He that overcometh, the same shall be
> clothed in white raiment; and I will not blot out his
> name out of the book of life, but I will confess his
> name before my Father, and before his angels.
>   . . .To him that overcometh will I grant to
> sit with me in my throne, even as I also overcame,
> and am set down with my Father in his throne.
> (Revelation 3:5, 21)

10
The Miracle of Healing

A man who had struggled with sin in his life shared a dream he had that helped him overcome the transgressions that had been a part of his past. In that dream, he entered a place where he saw, through an open doorway, a darkened, hazy bar where people were laughing and enjoying worldly pleasures. They seemed to be having a good time. For a moment, he felt drawn to them and thought of joining them, participating in their indulgences. Then he quickly decided, "No. I've decided against doing those things. I don't want that to be a part of my life anymore."

As he turned away from the doorway, he noticed a stairwell nearby. The light on the stairs seemed to grow with each successive step upward. He became curious about these stairs and decidedly turned toward them to begin an ascent to the top.

The nearer he approached the top of the stairs, the more clearly he could hear music that was being sung by a choir. The music almost beckoned him because of its beauty.

When he arrived at the top of the staircase, he could see a large crowd of spectators watching and listening to this choir sing. Surprisingly, the choir was small; there were "few singers and a lot of empty seats." Still, choir members sang powerfully. These people were singing under the direction of the choirmaster, who he sensed innately—and with certainty—was our Lord and Savior, Jesus Christ.

The music became so compelling that it soon became apparent he didn't solely want to be a spectator; he felt a deep desire to participate in the singing. In his longing to do this, he worked his way through the large crowd and finally approached the choir. He then sat on the ground near them, listening intently to the music. He knew he couldn't join them at that point in time because he "didn't know the words." He, therefore, sat on the ground and listened.

Finally, there was a woman who glanced over at him and saw him sitting on the floor. With one hand, she beckoned him to join her, and he got up and sat beside her. She then showed him the words to the song they had been singing, pointing at them in the book she held. From this gesture, this man became able to participate in the choir and began to sing. He now "knew the words."

Later on, this man found great spiritual significance in this dream. He came to believe that his wife, who had been a light and strength to him through his times of sin and transgression because of her faith in the Savior, was the woman who had shared her songbook with him and who had "taught him to sing." He feels his desire to become sanctified and cleanse his life came from her sharing the music of her testimony and love of the Savior—that it was because of her prayers, the "prayers of the righteous," that he was "spared." (Alma 10:23)

This miracle of healing can and has come to many couples who have or who are struggling through the consequences of sin and transgression. Those who align their wills to the will of our Heavenly Father can begin to taste of the healing power of our Savior in their lives. As President Howard

W. Hunter once said, "If Jesus lays His hands upon a marriage, it lives." (*Ensign*, Nov. 1979, p. 64)

One woman described the miracle of healing this way: "The path was never easy, but it was worth it—to see what my husband is today. It's amazing to watch what he has become. And my children now have their father."

Another woman compared the past pain and heartache of her husband's betrayal to memories associated with the difficulties of childbirth. "I can remember the pain of labor and how badly I felt giving birth, but it's become a faded memory to me. You do forget the intense pain associated with a betrayal. There is healing. I would never trade my husband for what he is today."

Many couples can testify that the healing of the Savior has come into broken, damaged relationships and made them whole once again. As Isaiah testified regarding the Savior:

> . . .The Lord hath anointed me to preach good tidings unto the meek; he hath sent me to bind up the brokenhearted;. . .to comfort all that mourn;
>
> To appoint unto them that mourn in Zion, to give unto them beauty for ashes, the oil of joy for mourning, the garment of praise for the spirit of heaviness;
>
> . . .Everlasting joy shall be unto them. (Isaiah 61:1-3, 7)

Truly the Savior can bring about "beauty for ashes" in relationships once damaged by sin.

Pearls in the Treasure Chest of Testimony

Many couples have come to believe, despite the hardships they've been through, that they would not forego past trials for the knowledge of the Savior that they've gained through difficult experiences. These pearls of insights and wisdom become priceless. They have come, like the people of Alma, to know "of a surety that I, the Lord God, do visit my people in their afflictions." (Mosiah 24:14) Many have experienced the promise that

> whosoever putteth his trust in him the same shall be lifted up at the last day. Yea, and thus it was with this people.
>
> For behold, I will show unto you that they were brought into bondage, and none could deliver them but the Lord their God, yea, even the God of Abraham and Isaac and of Jacob.
>
> And it came to pass that he did deliver them, and he did show forth his mighty power unto them, and *great were their rejoicings.* (Mosiah 23:22-24, italics added)

Many will testify again and again of the multiple times the Lord reached out in mercy and tenderness during times of struggle and heartache. For one woman, priesthood blessings became a tremendous source of counsel, strength and insight which helped greatly in her healing. She recalls one blessing where she had been told to "cling to the iron rod with both hands for those who are clinging to you," knowing this meant she needed to stay spiritually strong for her children and her husband who had been trying to overcome sin.

Another woman recalled after a time of intense darkness and struggle that a beautiful hymn played over and over in her mind. She was not familiar with this hymn but after a careful search through the hymnbook, she found that the music went to "Jesus, Lover of My Soul."

> *Jesus, lover of my soul,*
> *Let me to thy bosom fly,*
> *While the nearer waters roll,*
> *While the tempest still is high.*
> *Hide me, O my Savior, hide,*

Till the storm of life is past.
Safe into the haven guide;
Oh, receive my soul at last.

Other refuge have I none;
Hangs my helpless soul on thee.
Leave, oh, leave me not alone;
Still support and comfort me.
All my trust on thee is stayed;
All my help from thee I bring.
Cover my defenseless head
With the shadow of thy wing. (Hymns, 102)

She came to learn, as many others have, that the Lord will never forsake His children—especially during times of heartache and struggle. As it says in Isaiah 44:

> I will pour water upon him that is thirsty, and floods upon the dry ground: I will pour my spirit upon thy seed, and my blessing upon thine offspring:
> . . .O Israel, thou shalt not be forgotten of me.
> I have blotted out, as a thick cloud, thy transgressions, and, as a cloud, thy sins: return unto me; for I have redeemed thee.
> Sing, O ye heavens; for the Lord hath done it; shout, ye lower parts of the earth: break forth into singing, ye mountains, O forest, and every tree therein: for the Lord hath redeemed Jacob, and glorified himself in Israel. (3, 21-23)

Alma 38:5 promises, "As much as ye shall put your trust in God even so much ye shall be delivered out of your trials, and your troubles, and your afflictions, and ye shall be lifted up at the last day."

The scriptures also claim: "God shall wipe away all tears from their eyes; and there shall be no more death, neither sorrow, nor crying, neither shall there be any more pain: for the former things are passed away. . . .He that overcometh shall inherit all things; and I will be his God, and he shall be my son." (Revelation 21:4, 7)

"Clean Every Whit" (John 13:10)

Many transgressors have come to taste of the Savior's power to deliver them from the pain of past sins and decisions. Like Zeezrom, whose mind had been "harrow(ed) up until it did became exceedingly sore, having no deliverance" because of "his iniquity" and "many. . .sins," they too have been recipients of the Lord's mercy and "the power of Christ unto salvation" and have been healed "according to [their] faith which is in Christ." (Alma 15:3, 6, 10)

President Spencer W. Kimball said this of cleansing:

> When a physical body is filthy, the process of cleansing is a thorough bath, the brushing of teeth, the shampooing of hair, the cleaning of fingernails, and the donning of fresh clean clothing. . . .When a defiled man is born again, his habits are changed, his thoughts cleansed, his attitudes regenerated and elevated, his activities put in total order, and everything about him that was dirty, degenerate or reprobate is washed and made clean.
>
> . . .The effect of the cleansing is beautiful. These troubled souls have found peace. These soiled robes have been cleansed to spotlessness. These people formerly defiled, having been cleansed through their repentance—their washing, their purging, their whitening—are made worthy for constant temple service and to be found before the throne of God associating with divine royalty. (*Miracle of Forgiveness*, pp. 352-353)

One woman, who dealt with a husband who had been

trapped by a pornography addiction, came to compare this cleansing and overcoming of sin—and the overcoming of sin of other transgressors—to a flower she had seen growing out of a rock as a young child. She remembered upon first seeing the flower, she thought, "How is that possible?" As she looked closer at it, she could see a tiny crack that the flower had worked its way through to become strong, vibrant and beautiful.

She compared this to those transgressors who have had to overcome great obstacles to become what they are. They have grown and reached heights many others could not have reached given the same circumstances. She now feels a depth of love and appreciation for these amazing "flowers" who have overcome to become beautiful and strong. "Therefore they did forsake all their sins, and their abominations, and their whoredoms, and did serve God with all diligence, day and night," the scriptures tell us. (3rd Nephi 5:3)

Once this happens, these transgressors can come to trust in the divine promise in Ezekiel that, if they "turn from [their] sin(s), and do that which is lawful and right" and "walk in the statutes of life, without committing iniquity" that *none of [their] sins that [they] hath committed shall be mentioned unto [them]."* (Ezekiel 33:14-16, italics added) This great promise beautifully illustrates the Lord's abundant mercy available to all those who turn to Him to overcome the world through the power of His atoning sacrifice.

Allegory of the Olive Tree

The allegory of the olive tree in Jacob 5 can be used to aptly describe the miracle of healing in the lives of couples who have had to struggle through pornography addictions and have overcome them together. Many verses can be used to illustrate the Lord's tender mercies in His dealings with transgressors and those faithful servants who are called to work with them through this process.

In the first place, transgressors have been planted "in a

good spot of ground; yea, even that which was choice unto me above all other parts of the land of my vineyard," (v. 43) the Lord tells us. In other words, transgressors have been planted in places where the gospel has been taught and the gospel light has been available to them. The Lord knows their "roots are good" (v. 36) in that these men have valiant spirits who have good desires and intentions.

But the "loftiness" of these transgressors—their pride and haughtiness—have "overcome the roots which are good" and they have become "corrupted." (v. 48) Their behaviors and actions have become wicked. The Lord says of these transgressors that they "profit me nothing, and the roots thereof profit me nothing so long as [they] shall bring forth evil fruit." (v. 35)

The Lord feels deep sorrow for their wicked actions and evil behaviors.

> The Lord of the vineyard wept, and said unto the servant: What could I have done more for my vineyard?
>
> Behold, I knew that all the fruit of the vineyard, save it were these, had become corrupted. And now these which have once brought forth good fruit have also become corrupted; and now all the trees. . .are good for nothing save it to be hewn down and cast into the fire.
>
> And now, behold, notwithstanding all the care which we have taken of my vineyard, the trees thereof have become corrupted, that they bring forth no good fruit; and these I had hoped to preserve, to have laid up fruit thereof against the season, unto mine own self. But, behold, they have become like unto the wild olive-tree, and they are of no worth but to be hewn down and cast into the fire; and it grieveth me that I should lose them. (v. 41-42, 46)

He then claims he did everything He could so they would live righteously. "What could I have done more in my vineyard?" He asks once again.

> Have I slackened my hand, that I have not nourished it? Nay, I have nourished it, and I have digged about it, and I have pruned it, and I have dunged it; and I have stretched forth mine hand almost all the day long, and the end draweth nigh. And it grieveth me that I should hew down all the trees of my vineyard, and cast them into the fire that they should be burned. (v. 47)

The Lord then claims that these transgressors should be lost "except we should do something for [them] to preserve [them]." (v. 37)

Therefore, the Lord plants servants in their lives who will, along with the Lord, "labor with their mights" and who will "obey the commandments of the Lord of the vineyard in all things." (v. 72) Together the Lord and His servants work hard and long in these efforts to cleanse. They "graft" (v.54) and "pluck" (v. 52) that they may "preserve" the soul of the transgressor "that when they shall be sufficiently strong perhaps they may bring forth good fruit unto [the Lord], and [He] may yet have glory in the fruit of [His] vineyard." (v. 54)

This is a slow, gradual, arduous process, done in a specific time frame for both the transgressors and those surrounding him. The Lord counsels His servants, "Ye shall not clear away the bad thereof all at once, lest the roots thereof should be too strong for the graft, and the graft thereof shall perish, and I lose the trees of my vineyard." (v. 65)

The Lord continues, "Ye shall clear away the bad according as the good shall grow, that the root and the top may be equal in strength, until the good shall overcome the bad." (v. 66) Thus, "they shall be one." (v. 68) In other words, the Lord waits until His servants have become sufficiently strong in testimony and inward steel before He calls them to this work of overcoming the bad.

He then asks His servants to continue to labor "with all diligence." (v. 74) They do so labor insomuch that "there began to be the natural fruit again in the vineyard; and the natural branches began to grow and thrive exceedingly; and the wild branches began to be plucked off and to be cast away." (v. 73) They continue even until "the bad had been cast away out of the vineyard, and the Lord had preserved unto himself the natural fruit, which was most precious unto him from the beginning." (v. 74)

The Lord then calls His servants who have labored with Him and commends them for their diligent work. "Behold, for this last time have we nourished my vineyard; and thou beholdest that I have done according to my will; and I have preserved the natural fruit, that it is good, even like as it was in the beginning. And blessed art thou; for because ye have been diligent in laboring with me in my vineyard, and have kept my commandments, and have brought forth again unto me the natural fruit, that my vineyard is no more corrupted, and the bad is cast away, *behold ye shall have joy with me because of the fruit of my vineyard.*" (v. 75, italics added)

The Lord then promises that generations afterward will be blessed because of this great work. "For behold," He says, "for a long time will I lay up of the fruit of my vineyard unto mine own self. . .according to that which I have spoken." (v. 76) This all came about because of the diligent work of His faithful servants who labored with him in healing the fruit of His vineyard.

The Lord can truly effect this miracle of healing in the lives of transgressors when righteous and faithful servants work hand in hand with Him. He can and will help transgressors, their partners and children become pure, clean and whole again through His atoning power. "And then shall they rejoice; for they shall know that it is a blessing unto them from the hand of God; and their scales of darkness shall begin to fall from their eyes; and many generations shall not pass away among them, save they shall be a pure and a delightsome people." (2nd Nephi 30:6) Though this is talking about the Lamanites in the last days, it can assuredly apply to transgressors who cleanse lives and lineages through the redeeming power of our Lord and Savior, Jesus Christ.

> Let thy bowels also be full of charity towards all men, and to the household of faith, and let virtue garnish thy thoughts unceasingly; then shall thy confidence wax strong in the presence of God; and the doctrine of the priesthood shall distil upon thy soul as the dews from heaven.
>
> The Holy Ghost shall be thy constant companion, and thy scepter an unchanging scepter of righteousness and truth; and thy dominion shall be an everlasting dominion, and without compulsory means it shall flow unto thee forever and ever. (D&C 121:45-46)

"Return Unto Me. . .That I May Heal You" (3rd Nephi 9:13)

When our Savior tells us He has "overcome the world," (D&C 50:41), this means that He has. He has the power and capacity to overcome everything in it—every evil, every transgression, and every pain, heartache and sorrow. He can and He will. His healing and strength is a free gift for every needy soul who comes unto Him and builds upon this "sure foundation." (Helaman 5:12) He invites with outstretched arms, "Will ye not now return unto me, and repent of your sins, and be converted, that I may heal you?" (3rd Nephi 9:13)

One woman became deeply touched by an experience that showed her this healing power of the Savior. When she first learned that a transgressor she had loved had been granted the opportunity for re-baptism back into the church, her heart felt incredible peace, heartfelt relief and pervading joy. Simultaneously with these feelings and emotions came a beautiful impression into her mind which said, "The Lord's atonement is all-encompassing." She felt the burdens of all past heartaches, concerns and wounds lifted at that time through the amazing power of the Savior's atonement, and she felt to rejoice in the Savior's saving power and His tender mercy.

This type of experience can be illustrated in an event from Phil S.'s life in *The Perfect Brightness of Hope*. He recounts the time when he was to meet with a "well-known General Authority" to be interviewed and "if found worthy, to receive the Restoration of Blessings ordinance which would restore my Priesthood and temple blessings" after his excommunication.

"As the interview began," he writes, "this special man commented that he had participated in thousands of interviews to restore blessings." He continues in a journal entry dated February 13, 1989:

> He [the General Authority] had only one question—but it was most important. "Brother Phil, have you forgiven yourself?"
>
> *That's it? Only one question?* I thought, reflecting on my experience a year earlier. . . ."Yes," I replied. "I have forgiven myself."
>
> How precious was this gentle man. . . .I felt his goodness, his love, and his spirit, the familiar testimony of the Spirit. . .and I felt a deep love for him. He informed me that once my blessings were restored, the records of the Church would *never* indicate that I had lost membership. I thought of the scripture from Isaiah, *Though your sins be as scarlet, they shall be as white as snow* (Isaiah 1:18).
>
> He placed his hands on my head and restored my Priesthood and temple blessings and gave me a powerful blessing of comfort and counsel. I listened carefully, intent on remembering as much as possible. . . .As the blessing progressed, I began to feel a profound transformation. I felt God's power through the Priesthood flowing into me. I felt this power radiating down through the hands of this pure man and into my body. I know that Priesthood and temple endowment are tangible properties. I

felt them there at that moment. I recognized this feeling like the companionship of an old friend, the wonderful witness from the Holy Ghost giving ultimate proof of the truth. I felt within me the power of the Priesthood of God—it was now mine again! I had my temple blessings back! I again had the promise that I could receive *all God has* if I continued faithful. (pp. 145-147)

His mother wrote to him shortly after this experience and said:

When I saw a man coming through the front door. . .dressed in a suit and white shirt, my heart leaped within me. I knew immediately it was you. As you approached, there was a glow all about you, but especially about your head—almost like a halo. I didn't have to ask if your Priesthood and temple blessings had been restored. Even from a distance, I knew they had! I felt it with assurance as you hugged me.

There is no greater joy for a mother than to have a child who was lost return Home. With the same measure of despair that I shared the darkness and sorrow of your life over the past years of struggle, my soul now rejoices in the light of your return. I share your joy, for it is mine also! (p. 148)

When we come to taste of the Lord's redeeming and saving power in this way, we will echo the words of Neal A. Maxwell when he said: "Our gratitude for Christ and the atonement will grow with the years and the decades. It will never cease growing. And the scriptures foretell that *we will praise him forever and ever* (see D&C 133:52)." (*Ensign*, Oct. 2001, p. 10, italics added) We will indeed praise our Savior forever and ever for the tender love, compassion and mercy that He extends to those trying with everything they have to overcome the stain of sin in their lives, and those trying to help them through this difficult process. We humbly bear testimony of this, and we confirm Ammon's words when he said:

> Blessed be the name of our God; let us sing to his praise, yea, let us give thanks to his holy name, for he doth work righteousness forever.
>
> . . .We have reason to praise him forever, for he is the Most High God, and has loosed our brethren from the chains of hell.
>
> . . .Therefore, let us glory, yea, we will glory in the Lord; yea, we will rejoice, for our joy is full; ye we will praise our God forever. . . .Who can say too much of his great power, and of his mercy, and of his long-suffering toward the children of men?
>
> . . .He has all power, all wisdom, and all understanding; he comprehendeth all things, and he is a merciful Being, even unto salvation, to those who will repent and believe on his name.
>
> . . .Now my brethren, we see that God is mindful of every people, whatsoever land they may be in; yea, he numbereth his people, and his bowels of mercy are over all the earth. Now this is my joy, and my great thanksgiving; yea, and I will give thanks unto my God forever. (Alma 26:8, 14, 16, 35, 37)

> Wherefore, be faithful; stand in the office which I have appointed unto you; succor the weak, lift up the hands which hang down, and strengthen the feeble knees.
>
> And if thou art faithful unto the end thou shalt have a crown of immortality, and eternal life in the mansions which I have prepared in the house of my Father. (D&C 81:5)

–Appendix–

Mothers: Beware
The Dangers of Pornography

It should be noted that almost all those who have become addicted to pornography started the tendency or predisposition in their early teen years—some even before this. Most often the precursor to pornography is not sexual desire but solely the satisfaction of "curiosity." Even slight exposures during this time can be harmful and begin to breed a desire that might become a consuming, overpowering lust down the road. (For example, one man traced his addiction to a suggestive poster he'd seen in a neighbor's home when he was ten years old.)

Intense caution needs to be made in exposure to movies, magazines, music, the internet, books, and any other forms of entertainment. Some addictions have even been ascribed to such things as "Victoria's Secret" or department store catalogues. Parents need to be watchful and careful about what enters their homes. They need to be vigilant about screening materials that will be seen by their children.

One woman described a dream she had which illustrates this concept. In her dream, two big, burly men came to her door and knocked, asking to come in. She kept her door chained as she opened it and began speaking to them. In their attempts to persuade her to let them in, she remembers distinctly having the feeling that if she let them in and they had evil intent toward her or her children, she would be the only one to confront them. They could easily overpower her physically. She knew her only safety remained in the fact that she would never let the door open and let them inside in the first place. Such is the case with pornography. Once it comes in, it can become a powerful, overwhelming influence not easily overcome, even with diligent effort. The best road to take is to not let pornography into the home at all.

Open and honest discussions of the dangers of pornography need to start with children even *before* entering teenage years. Masturbation has become a common problem both independently and in tandem with pornography and needs to be discussed openly, as well. As Vaughn J. Featherstone claimed, any boy who successfully avoids masturbation during his teen years "would be quite a rare young man." (*Ensign*, Nov. 1980, p. 87)

Bishops need to be scrutinizing in worthiness interviews regarding masturbation and pornography. As one Bishop said, he no longer asks if anyone has a "problem" with pornography. Even if that person participated in pornography the night before, he would say "no"—believing in his determination not to participate in pornography again. Instead, this Bishop becomes "assumptive." He asks, "*When* was the last time you looked at pornography?" Many, many confessions have come about through this approach, pinpointing behaviors that might become uncontrollable addictions later on if they had not come out in the open and been addressed.

It needs to be noted that young women are not immune to problems with masturbation and pornography. Masturbation has become an increasing problem among young women and needs to be openly discussed. Many modern romances and daytime soap operas can be considered "soft porn" and become addictive, as well, destroying virtuous thoughts, goals and ideas.

One woman spoke about her addiction to romance novels this way:

> Whether I admitted it to myself or not, I was addicted to pornographic literature. Almost every day I set aside worthy activities so that I could spend hours reading or fantasizing about what I had read. The more I did so, the easier it became for me to engage in other types of sinful behaviors and thoughts. I even came close to having an affair. Fortunately, the covenants I had made in the temple kept me from making that serious mistake. Yet I felt overwhelmed and sometimes out of control.
>
> . . .Finally I realized I was not gaining ground on my problem. I recognized my inadequacies and told the Lord I was helpless without Him. I begged Him to make me strong enough to rise above this temptation.
>
> . . .I don't remember when I received the peaceful assurance that, together, the Lord and I would win. . . .When I became fully committed to seeking the Lord's help, the freedom actually came quickly. What joy!
>
> . . .Often when we hear about the evils of pornography, we think of pornographic magazines, movies and Web sites. Because men are more visually oriented, such material seems to appeal primarily to them. Yet the sexually explicit literature targeted at women, who are more verbally oriented, can be damaging as well. Like visual pornography, such literature presents a warped view of sexuality and is arousing and addictive. It dulls our spiritual senses, which distances us from God, and it can impair our

ability to have healthy, lasting relationships.

Sexual sin of any degree can be difficult to overcome. But with the Lord's help, it can be conquered. How grateful I am for the Lord, who made repentance and forgiveness possible. (*Ensign*, July 2003, pp. 57-59)

Monitoring the dressing and behavior of young women, who do not often realize the effects their bodies have on young men, becomes an important element in safeguarding children, as well. Often young women don't realize how damaging provocative behaviors can be to young men during their formative years and how powerful their exposed bodies can be in terms of temptation. As Paul counsels in 1ˢᵗ Timothy, women should "adorn themselves in modest apparel, with shamefacedness and sobriety" in such a way as "becometh women professing godliness." (2:9-10)

Once parents come to understand the deadly dangers surrounding pornography, they need to be vigilant in their efforts to keep it from their lives and homes. They also need to have frank, honest and open discussions with their children, helping them understand that these temptations, if not avoided, will allow Satan to "lead them by the neck with a flaxen cord, until he bindeth them with his strong cords forever." (2 Nephi 26:22)

Be ye therefore followers of God, as dear children.

. . .But fornication, and all uncleanness, or covetousness, let it not be once named among you, as becometh saints;

. . For this ye know, that no whoremonger, nor unclean person, nor covetous man . . .hath any inheritance in the kingdom of Christ and of God.

Be not ye therefore partakers with them.

. . .For ye were sometimes darkness, but now are ye light in the Lord: walk as children of

light:
    And have no fellowship with the unfruitful
works of darkness, but rather reprove *them*.
(Ephesians 5:1-11)

NOTE: There is a Web site that can show if there has ever been any pornography pulled up on a computer—even "cookie" files that have been removed from the history list. It is a free service through *www.strengthenthefamily.net.* Click on *www.contentwatch.com* and use the option called "Content Audit." It will show every questionable site that has ever been on your computer. (Hamilton, *Strengthen the Family*, p. 86)